Why, God?

GREG LAURIE

Why, God?

ISBN: 978-0-9777103-9-3

Published by: Allen David Publishers—Dana Point, California

Coordination: FM Management, Ltd.

Cover design: Chris Laurie

Interior design: Highgate Cross+Cathey

Production: Highgate Cross+Cathey

Printed in the United States of America

Contents

⟨ONE⟩

Behind-the-Scenes of Suffering

Have you ever had a really bad day? Consider the plight of three janitors at Fowler Elementary School in Ceres, California. Alerted to the fact that there was a gopher loose in the building, these three vigilant custodians finally cornered the rodent in a utility room.

Some time later, after recovering from his injuries, one of them explained just what happened in that encounter. It seems that they tried to spray the rodent with several canisters of a solvent used to remove gum from floors, hoping to freeze it to death.

Believing their efforts successful, one janitor lit a cigarette in the poorly ventilated room. Sparks from the lighter ignited the solvent, and the ensuing explosion blew all three of them out of the room and injured sixteen students in the adjoining hallway. Fortunately no one was seriously injured. Not even the gopher. The little animal survived the incident and was released in a field.

Now that is called having a really bad day. Maybe you're having that kind of day even as you read this book. How would you know? I came across this list somewhere.

You know you are having a really bad day when...

- your pacemaker comes with a thirty-day money-back guarantee

- the pest exterminator climbs under your house and never comes out

- a copy of your birth certificate arrives in the mail marked "null and void"

- the restaurant gives you a senior discount without asking, and you're only thirty-seven years old

- your wife takes the dog on vacation and leaves you at the kennel

- your plants do better when you don't talk to them

- the bird singing outside of your window is a vulture

- your horn sticks on the freeway behind thirty-two Hell's Angels motorcyclists.

I'm reminded of a story of a woman whose husband was critically ill and had been slipping in and out of a coma for several months. Through it all, his wife of many years had faithfully stayed by his side every single day. One day he came to and motioned for his dear wife to come closer.

She nestled close, her eyes filled with tears.

"You know what?" he rasped. "You've been with me through all of the bad times. When I got fired, you were there to support me. When my business failed, you were there. When I got shot, you were right there by my side. When we lost the house, you didn't leave me. And when my health started failing, you were still by my side."

And then the husband said, "You know what?"

The wife drew a bit closer and said, "What?"

"I think you're bad luck."

We may laugh at that, but the fact is that you and I face trouble from the day we are born. It comes with the territory of life on a broken planet. In fact, if you ever find yourself experiencing a conflict-free day, you can chalk it up as one of the better and more rare days of your life.

Conflict is one thing. But what about those days when it seems like the bottom drops out? You know what I'm talking about. It's a day when what couldn't go wrong goes wrong, and then even more goes wrong beyond that. And you ask yourself, *Why is this happening to me?*

Or maybe you're watching the evening news, and it seems like events all over the world are spinning out of control. You hear about a deranged student shooting students and teacher, and you ask the question, "Why?" Why would someone do something like this? How could anyone be given over so totally to evil?

Or maybe you hear of a natural disaster like a tsunami or an earthquake wiping out thousands of lives in an instant. And again you say, "Why?"

Or maybe, just to bring it home a bit, a friend of yours driving home from church gets killed in a head-on collision with a drunk driver. Later you learn that the inebriated person survived.

Why do things like that happen?

Why Does God Allow It?

Why does God allow tragedy? We've all heard it stated in many ways. Why does He allow babies to be born with disabilities? Why does He permit wars to rage? Why does He seem to turn the other way when innocent people are being killed? What about all of the horrible injustices in our world? Hurricanes. Epidemics. Wildfires. Why do these horrible things afflict our world? If God can prevent such tragedies, why does He allow them to take place?

Here is the classic statement of the problem: Either God is all-powerful but He is not all good, therefore He doesn't stop evil. Or He is all good but He is not all-pow-erful, therefore He can't stop evil.

The general tendency is to blame all of the problems of the world on God, to say that God is the one who is responsible.

"If God is so good and loving," people will say, "why does He allow evil?" Now the first part of that question is based on a false premise. By even stating it in that way, what they're really saying is that they don't believe God to be good and loving.

By questioning God's goodness and love, we are in essence saying that we can define goodness on our own terms. The fact is, God doesn't become good because that's our opinion of Him, or because we happen to per-sonally agree with His actions or His words. Nor does He become good because we vote on it and all agree that He is. God is good because God says He is good, and it's not up for a vote.

Jesus said, "No one is good—except God alone."[1] You see, God is good whether I believe it or not, and He alone is the final court of arbitration. As the apostle Paul said, "Let God be true but every man a liar."[2]

What, then, is "good"? Good is whatever God ap-proves. And by the same token, bad is exactly what God says is bad. Some might say that's circular reasoning. Yes, you could say that. But I would describe it as biblical rea-soning. The Word of God is our source of truth, defining right and wrong, and what our values ought to be.

In Isaiah 1:18 we read: "'Come now, let us reason together,' says the LORD." Or as another translation puts it, "Let's argue this out."[3] God is saying, "Here's the way I see things. You need to see it the way that I see it."

And He goes on to tell us that His thoughts are above our thoughts and His ways are above our ways. So God is good. Period.

Let's come back to the second part of that question. Why does He allow evil? The first thing we have to remember is that mankind was not created evil. Man and woman were created innocent... ageless... immortal. Their responsibility in the Garden of Eden was to tend it, watch over it, and discover all that God had created. But of course we know that our first parents made the wrong choice, ate the forbidden fruit, and changed everything down to this day.

But don't be too hard on Adam and Eve, because if you had been in the Garden, you would have done the same thing. And so would I. We might have fallen sooner or we might have fallen later, but we would have surely gotten around to it, as evidenced by the fact that we all make wrong choices throughout our lives.

The result of that original sin (we know all too well) was that death entered into the human race. As we are told in Romans 5:12 (NLT), "When Adam sinned, sin entered the world. Adam's sin brought death, so death spread to everyone, for everyone sinned." We need to keep in mind that humanity, not God, is responsible for sin.

In light of that, one might then ask the question, "Why didn't God make us incapable of sin?" Answer: Because He didn't want puppets on a string. He didn't want wind-up robots. He didn't want preprogrammed people with neither choice nor will.

I have a little granddaughter named Stella, and she's the apple of my eye. Not long ago she was over at our house with her mom and dad, and my wife and I were playing some little games with her—or, as much of a game as you can play with an eight-month-old baby. One of her toys played a little song, and Stella was kind of bopping to the beat (amazing child!).

As she was moving around, every few beats she would turn over and reach out her hand to me and wait for me to grab it. After we touched hands, she would turn around a few more times and then reach out her hand to me again. She did this about eight or nine times. And I loved it. I could have played that little game all day long. It was so cute, and it was just her little idea. She wouldn't stop reaching until I grabbed her tiny hand.

Now think about it. Stella didn't play that little game with me because I forced her to. She did it because I'm the greatest grandfather that ever was! (She doesn't know that yet, but she will.) This was something that came from her own will. She wanted to play a game and reach out her hand to me.

It's the same in our relationship with God. He doesn't want you to relate to Him and talk to Him and love Him because you have to. He wants you to do it because you choose to. He gave you that ability.

In the Garden, Adam and Eve used that independent will to make a wrong choice. So do we. Much of the evil in the world and the wrongs that are done are the result of wrong choices, one after another.

"Okay," you reply, "I can accept that. But why does God allow bad things to happen to good people? And more to the point, why does God allow bad things to happen to godly people?"

I'm glad you asked. Because that brings us to one of the greatest—and most tragic—stories in all the Bible. The book of Job is in God's Word for a reason, actually many reasons. But one of the principal things this book does is to help us think through this whole issue of the goodness of God and how it touches a world and a human race under the curse of sin.

Most of us can accept the idea of suffering in general, especially as an outcome or consequence of bad behavior. In other words, if someone lives a reckless, wicked life, committing horrible atrocities, and faces the repercussions of those deeds, we say, "They got what they deserved. It was poetic justice. They reaped what they sowed, and it finally caught up to them." We can accept the idea of suffering in circumstances like those. But how does it strike us when an innocent and godly person suffers?

That was the case with Job, a man who not only avoided doing wrong, but also worked very hard to do what was right. So much so, in fact, that God actually bragged about his righteousness and integrity before the hosts of heaven.

That was right before the bottom dropped out of Job's life, and everything changed. Maybe you've heard people talk about "the patience of Job." In the next few pages, we're going to see exactly what that statement means.

The Man from Uz

Job was a real, historical, flesh-and-blood man who many scholars feel walked the earth during the time of the patriarchs, somewhere between 2000 and 1800 BC. Scripture says he lived in the land of Uz—which may sound like Oz, but Uz was a real place in the world, not an imaginary land of munchkins and talking scarecrows. It was most likely east of the Jordan, perhaps in northern Arabia.

Many scholars tell us that the book of Job may be the oldest book of the Bible, possibly written by Moses himself.

The New Testament writer James validates Job's story and the great lesson it teaches about patience and faith:

We give great honor to those who endure under suffering. Job is an example of a man who endured patiently. From his experience we see how the Lord's plan finally ended in good, for he is full of tenderness and mercy. (James 5:11, NLT)

Uz was a real place, and Job was a real man with real problems with a real God to whom he turned—the very same God you and I can turn to in our times of need. Let's set the stage for this amazing account by picking up an introduction from Job chapter one.

There once was a man named Job who lived in the land of Uz. He was blameless—a man of complete integrity. He feared God and stayed away from evil. He had seven sons and three daughters. He owned 7,000 sheep, 3,000 camels, 500 teams of oxen, and 500 female donkeys. He also had many servants. He was, in fact, the richest person in that entire area.

Job's sons would take turns preparing feasts in their homes, and they would also invite their three sisters to celebrate with them. When these celebrations ended— sometimes after several days—Job would purify his children. He would get up early in the morning and offer a burnt offering for each of them. For Job said to himself, "Perhaps my children have sinned and have cursed God in their hearts." This was Job's regular practice. (Job 1:1-5, NLT)

So right off the bat we learn some important things about the man named Job.

#1: He was a man of integrity and character.

Character may be the most important thing in any individual's life. How do you determine character? Here's what it comes down to. When you are all alone, when no one is looking, when there's no one around to impress, what does your life look like? That is who you really are. The measure of a man or woman's real character is what they would do if they knew they would never be found out.

What if I could give you a foolproof guarantee that you could get away with a certain sin? Would you do it? Would you cheat on your income taxes? Would you be unfaithful to your spouse? If that is the case, then that is who you most truly are.

It really comes down to what you think about most. What saddens you? What makes you mad? What makes you laugh? That is your character. A German proverb says, "a man shows his character by what he laughs at."

The bottom line is that Job practiced what he preached. He was a man of true integrity. God Himself said so, and no one could have a higher endorsement than that.

#2: He was a wealthy man.

Success has turned many a head, and wealth has been a spiritual stumbling block to many. We are warned in Psalm 62:10, "If riches increase, do not set your heart on them."

Remember what Jesus said about wealth in the parable of the sower? He spoke of seed that was sown on the ground, where it took root but was eventually choked out by weeds. "The seed that fell among the thorns," Jesus explained, "represents [those] who hear God's word, but all too quickly the message is crowded out by the worries of this life, the lure of wealth, and the desire for other things, so no fruit is produced" (Mark 4:18-19, NLT).

That is not to say it is wrong to desire success, a nice home, or a prosperous business. But it is wrong if you let those things become the driving force in life. Don't let them become your obsession. Don't let them become your god. Because the Bible says, "Put to death, therefore, whatever belongs to your earthly nature: sexual immorality, impurity, lust, evil desires and greed, which is idolatry."[4]

Job had vast wealth and holdings, but it didn't turn his head.

#3: He was a family man.

Job raised his children in the way of the Lord and brought them before God in prayer every day without fail. Even when his adult kids were having a celebration, he would pray for them. He would offer a sacrifice on their behalf, which was an Old Testament way of saying he was interceding for them. Here was a dad who was concerned about the spiritual lives of his kids, and prayed every day that they would steer clear of sin and walk with God.

Our kids need our prayers every day of their lives, especially in the culture in which we live today. While it's true that we need to work toward releasing our sons and daughters and launch them into independent, self-sufficient lives, we'll always be their parents, and they will always need Mom and Dad's faithful prayers. Job was a concerned parent, bringing his family before the Lord and praying for their protection and blessing.

#4: He was a prayerful man.

When Scripture says Job prayed for his adult children, it underlines the fact that "this was Job's regular practice." In other words, when it came to prayer, Job wasn't hit-or-miss. He had an established routine of coming before the Lord with his requests.

The Bible says that we should "pray without ceasing" and "in everything give thanks, for this is the will of God in Christ Jesus for you."[5] Does that describe your life? Is God first in your list of priorities? Do you pray for your children? Do you set a godly example for them to follow? You've heard the expression "the apple doesn't fall far from the tree." That is so often true when it comes to loving the Lord and following Him. Your sons and daughters will take their cues from watching how you relate to God and the priority you give to your spiritual life.

Job set an outstanding example for his children. And as this story unfolds, we are given dramatic evidence as to why it's so vital to cover your family with prayer every day. In one of the most fascinating passages in all of Scripture, we are allowed to look behind-the-scenes and see what was happening in the spiritual realm that would directly affect Job's life and every member of his family.

Behind-the-Scenes

One day the members of the heavenly court came to present themselves before the LORD, and the Accuser, Satan, came with them. "Where have you come from?" the LORD asked Satan.

And Satan answered the LORD, "I have been patrolling the earth, watching everything that's going on."

*Then the LORD asked Satan, "Have you noticed my
servant Job? He is the finest man in all the earth. He is
blameless—a man of complete integrity. He fears God
and stays away from evil."*

*Satan replied to the LORD, "Yes, but Job has good
reason to fear God. You have always put a wall of
protection around him and his home and his property.
You have made him prosper in everything he does.
Look how rich he is! But reach out and take away
everything he has, and he will surely curse you to your
face!"*

*"All right, you may test him," the LORD said to Satan.
"Do whatever you want with everything he possesses,
but don't harm him physically." So Satan left the
LORD's presence. (Job 1:6-12, NLT)*

Talk about having friends—and enemies—in high
places! God was so proud of Job He was bragging on him.
Look again at verse 8. "Have you noticed my servant Job?
He is the finest man in all the earth. He is blameless—a
man of complete integrity."

When I read that statement and then go on to read
what happened to Job immediately after God made it, I
feel a little nervous about the idea of God ever bragging
on me! I almost feel like saying, "Lord if You're ever feeling proud of me just for a fleeting moment, could we kind
of keep it between the two of us?"

I wonder if God would ever boast of His servant Greg,
or would boast of you, with all the angels standing around.
I tend to doubt it in my case. We often will see ourselves
one way—maybe in a quick surface way—while God
knows us through and through. Over in the book of

1 Samuel we're told, "The LORD does not see as man sees; for man looks at the outward appearance, but the LORD looks at the heart" (1 Samuel 16:7).

You and I can be way off in the way we evaluate one another. We might be in a worship service and find ourselves drawing conclusions about how spiritual that person next to us is. If he's singing loudly, closing his eyes, and raising his hands up high, we might conclude, "Now that is a spiritual person." Then we look around a little more and see someone else who isn't singing at all. Maybe her head is bowed a little, but she's simply holding the chair in front of her and doesn't seem engaged in the worship. And we conclude, "She's not a very spiritual person. I wonder if she's even a believer." But the truth might be the very opposite of what we think!

We don't know what's going on in the heart of another person. So we had better leave all such conclusions and evaluations with the Lord Himself, where they actually belong. We need to just concentrate on seeking to live a godly life.

So here is God bragging on the man from Uz, calling him "My servant Job." There could be no higher endorsement, and no higher job description: a servant of the living God.

We're also introduced to Satan in this passage. We have to get rid of the world's stereotypical caricature of a devil in a red suit and pointed ears, wearing a goatee and carrying a pitchfork. (I especially take issue with the goatee part, as I have been known to sport one myself from time to time.) I'm not sure where that image came from, but it bears no resemblance to the description of our adversary in Scripture. Satan is a powerful spirit being. He is not a myth, not a cartoon character, and not "the dark side of the force," lacking identity or personality. He is real, and Scripture calls him by name.

... the Accuser, Satan, came... (Job 1:6)

... Satan answered... (Job 1:7)

In verse 7 he describes his activities to the Lord: "I have been patrolling the earth, watching everything that's going on." Then in verse 12 we read that Satan left the Lord's presence. You see, we're talking about an active personality with an agenda here, not an impersonal force. Satan has something he very much wants to accomplish.

And what is that? The devil's single, consuming ambition is to turn you and me away from God and all that is good. His ultimate agenda can be summed up in the statement of Christ in John 10:10, where Jesus said, "The thief does not come except to steal, and to kill, and to destroy. I have come that they may have life, and that they may have it more abundantly" (NLT).

You can immediately see the contrast. Jesus is in effect saying, "I have come to give you life. Satan has come to give you death. I have come to give you freedom. He has come to give you bondage. I have come to build you up, to save you, to restore you. He has come to steal, kill, and destroy." And that is what he wants to do to you this very day, this very hour.

Master Deceiver

The devil is very effective at what he does. Never doubt that. Never underestimate his capacity to package his wares, making bad things look good and good things look bad. He is a master deceiver, and we should never dismiss him or treat him lightly.

One wonders, why did God create someone as wicked as the devil to begin with? He didn't! God did not create Satan as we know him today. In fact, he was created as a beautiful and high-ranking angel named Lucifer, or "son of the morning." Once serving the Lord in a place of exalted glory and responsibility, Lucifer was in an elite category with other high-ranking angels like Michael and Gabriel. The book of Isaiah gives us a quick peek at what happened to this mighty being.

> *"How you are fallen from heaven,*
> *O Lucifer, son of the morning!*
> *How you are cut down to the ground,*
> *You who weakened the nations!*
> *For you have said in your heart:*
> *'I will ascend into heaven,*
> *I will exalt my throne above the stars of God;*
> *I will also sit on the mount of the congregation*
> *On the farthest sides of the north;*
> *I will ascend above the heights of the clouds,*
> *I will be like the Most High.'*
> *Yet you shall be brought down to Sheol,*
> *To the lowest depths of the Pit."*
> (Isaiah 14:12-15)

Lucifer, you see, was not satisfied with worshipping God. He wanted that worship for himself. So this once beautiful, powerful angel of God lost his exalted position in heaven. Lucifer became Satan when he fell to the earth. Satan means "accuser," which he now is. Jesus said, "I saw Satan fall like lightning from heaven."[6]

Now an enemy of God, Satan—along with his hosts of fallen angels—has many strategies to seduce, subvert, and destroy the people of God. He may approach us in all his depravity, seeking to draw us directly into his web of wickedness and sin. But the Bible says he can also appear as "an angel of light," seeking to deceive us and lead us off into false directions and wrong paths.

So even though we shouldn't become overly preoccupied with our adversary and his activities, it is wise for us to understand his methods of operation. Paul wrote to the Corinthians that they should take a certain course of action "in order that Satan might not outwit us. For we are not unaware of his schemes."[7]

Being aware of his schemes and how he operates can help us to effectively resist him. And that is exactly what Scripture tells us to do: "Resist the devil and he will flee from you" (James 4:7).

It would be one thing to deal with this one powerful spirit being. But the Bible tells us that when the devil fell, he did not fall alone. We're told in Revelation 12:4 that he took one-third of the angels with him—untold thousands of them. And it is my belief that those fallen angels are what we know as demons today, spirits that do his bidding and his dirty work. But though the devil lost his once-exalted position, we learn from this first chapter of Job that he still has access to heaven and the throne of God.

And what does he do with this access? He comes before God to accuse us. In fact, the Bible calls him "the accuser of our brethren."[8] The devil's primary objective in coming before the God of heaven is to bring constant and specific accusations against you and me and all followers of Jesus Christ.

That seems to be what is happening as Job's story opens.

Looking for Trouble

God says to Satan, "Where have you come from?" The devil responds, "I have been patrolling the earth, watching everything that's going on."

The Bible describes Satan as a roaring lion[9] walking about seeking whom he may devour. He never takes a vacation. He never rests. Wouldn't it be nice if the devil took a day off? A devil-free day. But it isn't going to happen. He doesn't take a day off—or an hour off or even a minute off. When he is defeated, he circles around and comes back for more. If you block him at the front door, he'll try to come in the back door, or sneak in through a window. If you keep your doors and windows shut, he'll try to come down through the ceiling or tunnel up through the floor. He is so persistent. He doesn't back off. He is like a lion constantly pursuing its prey.

We've all seen those programs on television where the zebras are running together, and there is that one little zebra lagging behind. As soon as you see him, you know he's a goner for sure. You feel so bad for him. "Oh, no! Get away, little zebra! Run faster!" But you know he's going to end up being a striped lunch for Leo the lion.

Satan walks to and fro, up and down, constantly sizing things up. He says, "There's a Christian who isolates himself from the other Christians. Maybe I'll go after him." Or, "There's someone filled with pride and arrogance. I know I can bring him down." Or, "Oh, that girl over there looks vulnerable right now. I know how I will defeat her. I'm moving in!"

He is always sizing you up. Always looking for a weakness. Always looking for a vulnerability of some kind. He is going back and forth across the earth just looking for trouble.

Jesus called Satan the father of lies.[10] But he also tells the truth sometimes, as in Job 1:9-10: "Job has good reason to fear God. You have always put a wall of protection around him and his home and his property. You have made him prosper in everything he does. Look how rich he is!" (NLT). The King James Version translates it this way: "You have put a hedge around him."

This brings us to a very important truth. Despite his heartless, wicked agenda, Satan still has to ask permission before he can touch a child of God. Why? Because of the hedge of protection that God has placed around each of his children. In one story in the Gospels, a host of demons even had to ask Jesus' permission to enter a herd of pigs!

Satan cannot simply ride roughshod over you and do whatever he wants, because God has placed limits on his activities. God knows our breaking point, and He will never give us more than we can take. In 1 Corinthians 10:13, Paul writes these crucial words: "No temptation has overtaken you except such as is common to man; but God is faithful, who will not allow you to be tempted beyond what you are able, but with the temptation will also make the way of escape, that you may be able to bear it."

There is always a way out. There is always a back door. Sometimes even the front door, or perhaps a window. You may think you are trapped and that there is no way out of Satan's web, but there always is! The enemy may harass you, but he can never exceed what God in His grace and wisdom allows.

On another occasion Satan came asking for permission to assault Simon Peter. Jesus turned to the fisherman and said, essentially, "Simon, Simon, Satan has been asking for you by name that you would be taken out of the care and protection of God."[11]

It's interesting that Satan asked specifically for Peter. Has he ever asked for me by name? I doubt it. I don't know that I have ever been tempted by the devil. You may be saying, "What do you mean by that, Greg? That's a strange statement." Let me explain. I have certainly been hit with temptations orchestrated by the devil, but Satan can only be in one place at a time. Sometimes we think of him as roughly God's equal, only on the dark side. We know that God is all-powerful, all-knowing, and everywhere-present, and we may imagine Satan to have similar attributes.

He doesn't. The devil is not God's equal. The devil is a powerful spirit being, but he has limitations. He can't be all over the world tempting and harassing everyone at the same time. That's why he employs his vast army of demons. So even though Satan himself may have never tried to tempt me and drag me down, he's had lots of help over the years. So in effect, it's the same thing. In the case of Peter, however, the devil didn't want to trust an attack to one of his underlings. He came knocking himself. Peter was a big fish, and a direct threat to Satan's kingdom.

Immediately aware of Satan's designs, Jesus warned Peter, assuring him, "I have prayed for you, Peter, that your faith would not fail."

Jesus prays for you, too. He is your Advocate, and speaks in your defense when the evil one tries to slander you before the Father. One popular paraphrase puts it like this:

I write this, dear children, to guide you out of sin. But if anyone does sin, we have a Priest-Friend in the presence of the Father: Jesus Christ, righteous Jesus.[12]

God has placed a hedge around you, an impregnable fortress that Satan and his demons cannot penetrate. Whatever comes your way, then, must be by God's permission. Just as God protected Job, so He will protect you.

You might ask the question, "Well, what if this or what if that happens? I saw this tragedy befall a friend of mine, and I couldn't handle that if that happened to me." That's likely true. Right at this moment, you couldn't handle it. But if God allowed that particular circumstance in your life, He would also give you the strength to endure it.

Attacking Job's Integrity

In the first chapter of Job, Satan says to God, in essence, "Job fears You, God, because You have given him a lot of wonderful possessions. But if you took it all away, he wouldn't fear You anymore. In fact, he would curse You to Your face. I can prove it to You, if You let me."

The Lord replies, "All right. But you can't touch him physically. Only those things that belong to him." That's a loose paraphrase, but it does give us a clear picture of Satan in his role as "the accuser of the brethren."

"Job? He's just a mercenary! He's just in it for what he can get out of it." Here's what that might look like in our lives. First, the devil whispers in your ear, "Go ahead and do it. You'll get away with it. No one will ever know. It'll be fun." So you do whatever it is he is enticing you to do. Then he comes back to you and says, "Why, you pathetic, miserable hypocrite! What a loser you are! You're worthless. God doesn't love you anymore, and your salvation is out the window. Don't show your ugly face in the church again. And don't even think about praying or reading the Bible!"

It's very easy to fall for this. And we find ourselves with our chin on our chest, kicking dirt, and saying, "Oh, Lord, I failed You. I'm not worthy to worship You and speak for You."

But wait. Hold on a minute here. You were never worthy. None of us were. None of us are. Even on your best day when you are doing everything right and don't commit any sins that you know of, you aren't even close to "worthy" on that day.

The devil doesn't want you to know that. He wants you to think, *Well, I've got to work my way back to God. I've got to do a bunch of good things if I'm going to approach the Lord in prayer.*

That is a lie.

You can approach God any time based on the sacrifice of Jesus on the cross and His blood shed for you. It has never been about your worthiness. It has always been about His grace extended to you.

When it comes to that, how much do we really understand about God's grace in Christ? Can we even begin to wrap our minds around it? The psalmist tried, using the biggest picture he could imagine.

As high as heaven is over the earth,
so strong is his love to those who fear him.
And as far as sunrise is from sunset,
he has separated us from our sins.[13]

The book of Hebrews says, "Let us therefore come boldly to the throne of grace, that we may obtain mercy and find grace to help in time of need" (Hebrews 4:16).

Once again, Satan doesn't want you to know these things. He doesn't want you to think about verses like these. No, he will whisper in your ear and say, "You've committed that sin one too many times. How many times do you expect God to forgive you? You can't go to Him." And then the guilt and despair will come—guilt that can drive you crazy.

Is all guilt bad? No, even guilt has its purpose. You might think of it as a warning system. You're walking down the street barefoot and you step on a little sliver of sharp glass. The pain in your foot shoots right up to your brain, and the warning is instantaneous. *Stop! Don't step down any further.*

It's just a little cut, and not all that bad. But it hurts. It is uncomfortable. It's not bad enough to have you check into the emergency room, but it's definitely reason to be careful, to back off a little. Yes, it slows you down for a minute or so, but it's definitely better than the alternative—which is putting your full weight on a large piece of glass, cutting your foot wide open, and having to go to the hospital to get stitched up.

Now, you don't like the discomfort of that initial pain, but it has served you well if it keeps you from more serious injury. Guilt can be the same way. When I say or do something wrong, I know it almost immediately. Guilt kicks in to say, "You are not right with God," or "You are not right with that person, and that needs to be rectified."

It's guilt. It's not enough to plunge me into despair or send me into depression, but it's enough to bring me to the cross, where I say, "Lord, I have failed. I have sinned in this, and I'm sorry. Please help me and forgive me."

As far as Satan is concerned, that's the worst. Everything in him wants to keep us from the cross, where Jesus paid the debt for our rebellion and sin with His own blood. It was the cross that sealed Satan's doom, and he doesn't want us anywhere near it. If he could, he would drive us far away from it. He wants us to feel guilty and condemned, separated from God. But God wants that guilt to bring us to Him, where we will find mercy, forgiveness, and healing.

Judas Iscariot sinned against Jesus by betraying Him, and then went out and hung himself. If Judas had sought forgiveness for his treachery, would Jesus have forgiven him? Yes, that's what I believe. And here's why. When Jesus was in the garden of Gethsemane, and Judas came with the temple guards to arrest Him, Jesus asked him, "Friend, why have you come?"

Did Jesus know why Judas had come that night? Of course He did. He had already identified him as the betrayer and told him to do what he was going to do quickly. But I believe in that final moment, Jesus was offering Judas one last opportunity to repent. But Judas listened to the wrong voice, the voice of guilt, and took his own life.

What about Peter? After he had denied the Lord, and then had direct eye contact with Him, Peter went out and wept bitterly. But here's the difference—he came back. Peter returned to Christ and was forgiven, restored, and offered an even wider, more significant ministry.

So here's the important lesson. If you fail the Lord (and you will), don't run from Him or try to hide. Come back to Him.

When Jesus said, "Simon, Simon! Indeed, Satan has asked for you, that he may sift you as wheat...", He added, "But I have prayed for you, that your faith should not fail; and when you have returned to Me, strengthen your brethren" (Luke 22:31-32).

You need to remember that your defense against the accusations of the devil is the Son of God Himself, who intercedes for you before the throne of the Father. He prays for you, He represents you, He defends you. Romans 8:33 (NIV) says, "Who will bring any charge against those whom God has chosen? It is God who justifies. Who is he that condemns? Christ Jesus, who died— more than that, who is raised to life—is at the right hand of God and is also interceding for us."

This is Jesus, our Savior. He is the One who saves us, justifies us, defends us, and preserves us. Yes, we believe and affirm these things. He is a faithful, merciful God, filled with lovingkindness.

But we're still left with a troubling question: Why would He allow righteous people to suffer? That's the question before us in the next chapter.

《TWO》

When Bad Things Happen to God's People

"Have a nice day."

We hear it a dozen times a day. The phrase is an American classic, isn't it? It often comes at the end of transaction at your local market, where the clerk will say, "Thank-you-for-shopping-with-us-and-have-a-nice-day." Do they mean it? Probably not, but it's in the employee manual, so they have to say it. For all the emotion and sincerity they put into it, they might as well be saying, "Cows eat grass."

Maybe you've stood at the returns window of your local big-box store, trying to return a defective or unwanted item for a refund. The employee behind the counter may very well say, "I'm sorry. We cannot accept your return. Have a nice day." How sorry are they? And how am I supposed to have a nice day when I'm stuck with an expensive but useless item?

What does it even mean to "have a nice day"? Does it mean a day devoid of all problems? A day free of all sickness, conflict, hardships, or speed bumps? Is that a "nice" day?

Sometimes God gets portrayed as nice, sort of a glorified Santa Claus, smiling benignly from heaven. He just wants everyone to get along, plant a tree, eat organic, and have a happy life. We can almost hear Him saying from

Mt. Sinai, "Have a nice day."

But is that really the picture that the Bible gives us? Is "niceness" one of His attributes as the true and living God? I'm not suggesting here that God can't or won't bless you with health or wealth. Nor am I suggesting that God is somehow reluctant to bring happiness into your life.

But it is not God's primary objective for you to have a nice day. God's objective in your life is to be glorified and to make you more like Jesus Christ. Your goal in life should not be happiness, but holiness. The good news is that one will follow the other! Truly holy people are among the happiest people you will ever meet. But to be a holy person means you will have to go through some trials, some hardships, and some suffering. It simply comes with the territory.

Now some would suggest that if you suffer, if you're sick, or if you're enduring some kind of hardship, it is a result of your own sin, and if you just had more faith this would not be happening to you. Those are wrong ideas, but they are not new ideas. That sort of false teaching goes all the way back to the oldest book of the Bible, the book of Job.

We read about the "behind-the-scenes" dialogue between God and Satan concerning Job's integrity and character. God had boasted about His servant, and Satan was hot to challenge the Lord's boast. What happened next was a string of events this good man couldn't have dreamed of in his worst nightmare.

The Darkest Day

One day when Job's sons and daughters were feasting at the oldest brother's house, a messenger arrived at Job's home with this news: "Your oxen were plowing, with the donkeys feeding beside them, when the Sabeans raided us. They stole all the animals and killed all the farmhands. I am the only one who escaped to tell you."

While he was still speaking, another messenger arrived with this news: "The fire of God has fallen from heaven and burned up your sheep and all the shepherds. I am the only one who escaped to tell you."

While he was still speaking, a third messenger arrived with this news: "Three bands of Chaldean raiders have stolen your camels and killed your servants. I am the only one who escaped to tell you."

While he was still speaking, another messenger arrived with this news: "Your sons and daughters were feasting in their oldest brother's home. Suddenly, a powerful wind swept in from the wilderness and hit the house on all sides. The house collapsed, and all your children are dead. I am the only one who escaped to tell you."

Job stood up and tore his robe in grief. Then he shaved his head and fell to the ground to worship. He said,

"I came naked from my mother's womb,
and I will be naked when I leave.

> *The LORD gave me what I had,*
> *and the LORD has taken it away.*
> *Praise the name of the LORD!"*
>
> *In all of this, Job did not sin by blaming God.*
> *(Job 1:13-22, NLT)*

Job was not having a nice day.

His losses in those horrific few hours are almost incomprehensible. Think about it. In one day Job, one of the wealthiest men in the land, lost everything—all his assets, so wisely and carefully built up through the years. His trusted servants—what we might call loyal, longtime employees—had all perished in a string of (what we know to be) supernatural disasters.

Those things would have been difficult enough to endure. But it got much, much worse. The worst news of all on this day was to hear that his children—his pride and joy—had all been killed. Seven sons and three daughters, wiped out in a moment.

Having walked with parents through the death of a child, I can tell you that this is the worst thing that can happen to a mother or a father. No parent ever wants to outlive his or her children. We spend our lives caring for them, nurturing them, loving them, and investing our hopes and dreams in them. For most loving fathers and mothers, to lose a child is a fate literally worse than death.

Satan had challenged God, saying, "You just let me take away the things he holds dear and then see how loyal and faithful Job will be. He'll curse You to Your face!"

The Lord granted Satan permission to turn Job's world upside down—within limits. The evil one would not be allowed to lay a finger on Job himself.

And how did Job fare in that attack? Did he curse God, as Satan suggested? No. He praised God. "The LORD gave me what I had, and the LORD has taken it away. Praise the name of the LORD!"

No wonder the Lord was bragging on Job! You can almost hear the pride in the Lord's voice as He says to Satan,

> "Have you noticed my servant Job? He is the finest man in all the earth. He is blameless—a man of complete integrity. He fears God and stays away from evil. And he has maintained his integrity, even though you urged me to harm him without cause."

But Satan wasn't through yet (is he ever?), issuing one final challenge.

> Satan replied to the LORD, "Skin for skin! A man will give up everything he has to save his life. But take away his health, and he will surely curse you to your face!"

> "All right, do with him as you please," the LORD said to Satan. "But spare his life." So Satan left the LORD's presence, and he struck Job with a terrible case of boils from head to foot."

> Then Job scraped his skin with a piece of broken pottery as he sat among the ashes. (Job 2:3-8, NLT)

In times like these, you would like to think you could turn to your spouse for support. But it didn't work that way for Job.

His wife said to him, "Are you still trying to maintain your integrity? Curse God and die."

But Job replied, "You talk like a foolish woman. Should we accept only good things from the hand of God and never anything bad?" (vv. 9-10).

We have much to learn from this story of Job. In his letter to the church, the apostle James wrote, "As you know, we consider blessed those who have persevered. You have heard of Job's perseverance and have seen what the Lord finally brought about. The Lord is full of compassion and mercy" (James 5:11, NLT).

Persevere. That's the key word here. The book of Job teaches us how to persevere—hang in there—when we go through heartaches and hard times. Because it's not a matter of *if* some kind of calamity, trial, sickness, or difficulty will strike you or someone you love—it's a matter of *when*.

From the pages of Job's story, we learn not only how persevere in our own dark days, but also how to bring comfort to others who are enduring times of great difficulty.

Satan's Unwitting Role

When we read about Satan, this powerful and evil spirit being who hates God and despises mankind, we might wonder why God allows Satan to even exist.

As he says in his own words, he is restlessly going back and forth across the earth, looking for trouble... looking for lives to ruin... looking for saints to stumble. In the last chapter we asked the question: Why does God allow him to carry on? Why doesn't the Lord just take him out?

Why? Well you might be surprised to know that Satan, in his own twisted way, serves the purposes of God. Just consider this: Satan unwittingly played a major role in the cross of Christ. In his enduring hatred for God's Son, the devil thought it would be a great idea to have Jesus betrayed, arrested, beaten within an inch of His life, and then crucified and put to death on a Roman cross.

Everything went according to Satan's plan. As Jesus told the mob who came to apprehend him, "This is your moment, the time when the power of darkness reigns."[14] The power of darkness did indeed reign that day, and Satan's plan succeeded.

But so did the plan of God. What the evil one didn't realize was that it was the Father's plan all along that the Messiah would die for the sins of the world. In the book of Zechariah and in Psalm 22, God even mentioned that the Messiah would die by crucifixion (graphically described thousands of years before it had even been invented).[15] In the prophecy of Isaiah, we're told "It was the Lord's will to crush him and cause him to suffer."[16] Unaware that he was making the biggest blunder since his rebellion against God, Satan played into the plan and purpose of God (also prophesied in the book of Zechariah) when in his rage and hatred he inspired Judas Iscariot to betray Jesus for 30 pieces of silver.[17]

Satan's "best shot" against God and the people of God was the crucifixion of the God-man, Jesus Christ. And in that act he unwittingly not only sealed his own doom, he opened the door for Jesus to offer redemption and salvation to the whole world.

But that's not the end of the matter. Believe it or not, Satan can also accomplish God's purposes through the trials and afflictions that he throws our way. How? By helping us to cling to the Lord in dependence and prayer and, as a result, grow stronger spiritually.

Company Shows Up

But let's think about Job's situation. He has lost his possessions. He has lost his children. He might have wished he had lost his wife after what she said, but she was still around, which only added to his misery. And on top of all that, he has broken out in ugly, painful boils. The one-time wealthiest, most influential man of his known world is reduced to sitting on an ash heap, scraping his scabs with fragments of a broken pot.

About that time, company showed up. The Bible names three friends who came to "sympathize with him and comfort him" (Job 2:11, NIV). As it turned out, Job would have been better off if these guys had just stayed home.

These three counselors apparently traveled a great distance, and when they arrived at Job's residence and caught sight of their old friend huddled out back on top of an ash heap, they were shocked right down to their sandals.

When they saw Job from a distance, they scarcely recognized him. Wailing loudly, they tore their robes and threw dust into the air over their heads to demonstrate their grief. Then they sat on the ground with him for seven days and nights. No one said a word to Job, for they saw that his suffering was too great for words. (Job 2:12-13, NLT)

Believe it or not, that was the perfect thing to do. What Job needed right then was just someone to be with him. These friends started out with the right idea when "no one said a word."

We need to learn from their example. When you spend time with someone who is suffering or grieving, don't feel that you need to necessarily say something "wise and profound" or try to explain the situation. To begin with, you don't know enough to explain anything, because that knowledge lies with God alone. And besides that, explanations have never healed a broken heart. Sometimes the best thing to do is just be there and say absolutely nothing.

When our Lord was facing His imminent arrest and crucifixion, He was waiting with His disciples in the garden of Gethsemane. To His three closest companions, Peter, James, and John, He said, "My soul is crushed with grief to the point of death." And then He said to them, "I want you to just stay with Me. Stay with Me and watch with Me."[18]

Watch with Me. He didn't ask for a sermon, He didn't want an explanation, and He wasn't looking for someone to step in and fix His situation. In His humanity and in His sorrow that night, He just wanted a few friends around, that's all. And they were with Him, at least in body. Unfortunately, they couldn't keep their eyes open and slept right through His great anguish and struggle.

When someone is hurting, you just need to go to them. One of the best things you can say is, "I don't know what to say." Then take your own advice and don't say anything! If you do say something, keep it simple.

"I love you."

"I'm here for you."

"I'm praying for you."

As a pastor, I frequently have to walk right into the middle of human suffering. And when I get that call that someone's child or spouse has died, or someone has found out they have cancer, it's very hard to deal with many times. Even pastors don't know what to say at these times.

But most of the time, my words aren't all that important anyway. I have found that by simply showing up—showing love and a readiness to listen—I've been able to bring comfort to these grieving ones. Sometimes you ask the individual what he or she is facing, and then you just close your mouth and listen with both ears.

A number of years ago, a man I know fairly well lost his daughter in a car accident. A month had passed since the accident, and I hadn't seen him since it happened. I happened to find myself in a room with him and a group of other guys, and though everyone knew about his daughter, they all tiptoed around the subject. No one said a thing to him or even approached him. It's almost as though he was being punished for suffering.

Why did these men hold back? They may have thought, *Well, if I say anything it might be real uncomfortable. He might even cry.* So no one was willing to even broach the subject.

I remembering thinking to myself, *Something needs to be said.* So I took him aside and just bumbled out the words, "I am so sorry about what happened to your daughter."

He looked me in the eyes and said, "Thank you for mentioning it," and began to open up. He just wanted someone to talk to! And sure he teared up, but that's part of the mourning process. When you have lost someone—a spouse, a parent, or a child—you don't want their passing to be simply swept under the rug. You don't want that loved one to be forgotten.

Many times, simply because they don't want to be uncomfortable, be rejected, or look silly, people keep their distance from those who grieve. Or if they do spend time with that individual, they will steer clear of mentioning the one who died.

That's no comfort at all. The grieving spouse or parent wants their loved one to be remembered. Sometimes you can simply say something like, "I miss John. I wish he was here with us right now. But thank God we will see him again in heaven."

You say, "Oh, I don't want to say that. They might cry."

Yes, they might. And a good cry might do them some good, too, as they are still dealing with the loss and mourning.

Many times we will say things that don't help at all, but actually deepen the sorrowing person's pain.

"I know how you feel..."

No you don't! So why say it?

"There's a reason for everything."

That may be true, but neither of you has any idea what that might be.

"Well, no one ever said life was fair."

What a rotten thing to say to someone in crisis!

"What doesn't kill us makes us stronger."

Now what idiot came up with that little gem?

"Well, cheer up. There's always someone worse off."

Believe it or not, I've heard that one many times. It has zero—no, negative—comfort value, and sounds about as callous as you can get.

"When life gives you lemons, make lemonade."

Say that and your friend will be seriously thinking about hurting you.

"Don't worry. Be happy."

Now they are thinking of killing you.

"Have a nice day."

Now they will kill you for sure.

We have to give people—even fellow believers—time and room to grieve their loss. Some people say, "She's with the Lord now. She's happier than she's ever been. Don't cry."

What do you mean, "Don't cry"? That's holding people to a higher standard than even the Lord does! The Bible says there is a time to laugh and a time to mourn.[19] Even Jesus wept at the tomb of His dear friend Lazarus. In the book of Acts, after Stephen was stoned to death by a violent mob, we read that devout men wept over him. It's okay to weep when you lose someone. But as the book of 1 Thessalonians says, we do not "grieve like the rest of men, who have no hope."[20] We do have hope. We have strong, unquenchable hope that we will be with our saved loved ones in heaven and share eternity together.

Job's comforters always get a bad rap, and deservedly so, but just remember something: *At least they got it right in the beginning.* They wept with their friend, kept their mouths closed, and sat with him on the ground for seven days before they said anything. We think we're being a martyr if we sit with someone for seven minutes. At least initially, Job's friends did the right thing. Scripture says to "Rejoice with those who rejoice, and weep with those who weep" (Romans 12:15).

Three Sorry Counselors

If Hollywood had written the book of Job, it would focus in on the supernatural connection, zero in on gory scenes of lightning strikes, terrorist raids, and natural disasters, then skip to the last chapter of the book. Anyone watching the movie would say, "What a great story. A man suffers huge losses, then God blesses him and restores much of what he lost."

The moviemakers would definitely skip all those long chapters filled with lame counsel from three loser friends. Yes, they had been mercifully silent for a while, but they more for made up for it later. And the conversation went on and on.

Let's focus in for a moment on the bill of goods each of these men tried to sell their grieving friend, Job.

Eliphaz

First there was Eliphaz, who saw God as inflexible and hard, always giving us just what we deserve.

> *"Stop and think! Do the innocent die? When have the upright been destroyed? My experience shows that those who plant trouble and cultivate evil will harvest the same. A breath from God destroys them. They vanish in a blast of his anger." (Job 4:7-9, NLT)*

Basically he is saying, "Job, I think you're just reaping what you've sown. You must have done some really bad things, and that's why this calamity has come upon you."

Now of course there is truth to the principle of reaping and sowing. There is cause and effect, and we've all seen the results of it. We see people who commit their lives to the Lord, begin to make wise decisions, and how their lives begin to turn for the better. And we also see those who make sinful, destructive choices, and observe with sorrow how they reap the bitter consequences of those sins.

But it doesn't always work that way. There are those inexplicable situations that go against all conventional

wisdom when the godly person—the man or woman who
has mostly made right choices throughout life—has to
undergo terrible suffering.

That was Job's case.

Bildad

Bildad basically said "ditto" to Eliphaz's stern lecture. He
too thought that bad things only happen to bad people,
and that Job's sorrows were the result of his own mis-
deeds.

"But look!" he said to Job. "God will not reject a
person of integrity, nor will he lend a hand to the wicked"
(8:20). In other words, "Job, if you were truly a man of
integrity this would not have happened." The irony of this
is that God Himself had declared Job a man of integrity.
We need to be very, very careful about passing judgment
on a person who is loved and treasured by God.

Zophar

Zophar was a real piece of work, even more blunt and
critical than his two buddies. He coldheartedly suggested
to Job that he was probably so sinful he deserved even
worse from the hand of the Lord! Here is Job, mourning
the loss of all he has, covered from head to toe with loath-
some boils, and Zophar declares, "Listen! God is doubt-
less punishing you far less than you deserve!" (11:6).

And then to add insult to injury, Zophar comes up with
this little gem of consolation in 20:6-8: "Though the pride
of the godless [speaking of Job] reaches to the heavens
and their heads touch the clouds, yet they will vanish
forever, thrown away like their own dung. Those who
knew him will ask, 'Where are they?' They will fade like a
dream and not be found" (NLT).

Wow. Thanks a lot, Zo. That's comforting.

Can you imagine Hallmark hiring these guys—Eliphaz, Bildad, and Zophar—to write sympathy cards?

Here is what Eliphaz's card would look like. On the cover it would say, "Sorry you are sick." Then you would open it up and it would read, "You got what you deserved."

Bildad's card would say on the outside, "Hoping you get well soon." Then on the inside it would say, "But if you were really godly this would never have happened."

But I think Zophar's card would have been the most brutal. I think on the cover it would have said, "I hope you get worse." Then on the inside it would read, "You will die, no one will remember you, and you will be thrown away like garbage."

If Job's wife sent him a card, the cover would read: "Why do you still trust God?" Then on the inside, "Why don't you curse Him and die? Love, your wife."

Not much comfort there.

The Question "Why?"

Much of the book of Job is dedicated to asking the question "why?"

Toward the end of the book, beginning in chapter 38, God finally responds to His suffering servant. It's evident the Lord was getting tired of all the lame explanations offered by Job's unhelpful friends—and of Job's own complaints and questions.

"Who is this that questions my wisdom with such ignorant words? Brace yourself like a man, because

I have some questions for you, and you must answer them." (vv. 2-3, NLT)

As God goes on speaking, He says in effect, "Excuse Me, but I guess I missed you when I was busy creating the universe. Were you there? I didn't notice you there." In this ironic sort of way, the Lord puts Job in his place and declares His own glory.

At the bottom line, I think the book ends up by saying that Job really didn't need an explanation of life and all its perplexities. What he needed was an encounter with God. What he needed was a fresh revelation of the Lord. Why? Because when we see God for who He is, we will see our problems for what they are. If we have a small God, we have big problems. But if we have a big God, we have small problems (no matter how huge and overwhelming they may seem to us).

All of this being said, you and I still see fellow Christians suffering—or maybe we're going through a deep valley of our own—and we can't help wondering why God allows this kind of pain and heartache in the life of a believer.

Why God Allows Christians to Suffer

Never, never forget that God is in control of all the circumstances that surround a believer's life. God is in control of your life, and involved in all the details. Your suffering has not escaped His notice. Your situation has not somehow been buried in His in-box. He is intimately aware of everything going on in your world, and no detail is too small to escape His attention. The word "oops" is not in God's vocabulary. And as we can so clearly see from the book of Job, the devil can do nothing in the life of the believer without the express permission of God.

Okay, you say, but if He's in control, why does He allow these hurtful things to happen to me and to people I love?

Here are some of the reasons why.

#1: Suffering makes us strong

The apostle James tells us,

> When all kinds of trials and temptations crowd into your lives my brothers, don't treat them as intruders, but as friends. Realize that they come to test your faith and produce in you a quality of endurance. And let that process go on until that endurance is fully developed. And you will find you have become men of mature character, men of integrity, with no weak spots.[21]

God allows hardship in our life so that our beliefs—those handholds of faith in a troubled world—will became more and more real to us, and less and less theory. We can start living out our faith-life in the real world.

I'm reminded of all the people you see on the road these days driving gleaming new SUVs. (We have one, too, by the way.) Most of these fancy rigs have 4x4 capabilities. In other words, you could drive them through the mud or power up some rocky track up a mountainside. But how many people really do that? I've certainly never taken my SUV out "four-wheeling."

Some guys, of course, take it a notch above that, putting lifts in their rigs and buying big, gnarly tires with huge lights mounted on the top. And what do they do with these powerful vehicles? They brag to their buddies, and say, "Yeah, just look at this thing. Look at what it can do. I could drive this baby up the side of a building."

"Well," someone might ask, "do you want to go out in the dirt?"

"Are you kidding? Do you know how much I paid for this thing? There is no way! In fact, I was just on the way to the car wash." They never want to actually use their vehicle for its intended purpose—what it was actually designed to do.

We can be that way with our beliefs. We talk about believing this and believing that, and the truths we hold dear. But I can hear God saying to us, "You know, you have a lot of really great beliefs. You talk about them all the time. I think it's time you started putting some of them into practice. You talk about how you trust Me. You talk about how you believe I can provide for your every need. Okay. Let Me put you in a situation where you have no other resources and really have to trust Me for that provision."

You see, God allows hardships and trials and shortfalls in our lives so that we will exercise our sometimes-flabby faith muscles and step out on trust alone. We need to transfer our faith from the realm of theory to in-the-trenches reality.

#2: Suffering can bring God glory

Any fool can be happy and peaceful when the sun shines down from a blue and cloudless sky. But when those qualities shine out from the midst of a dark and destructive storm, that's another matter entirely.

That, in essence, was the challenge Satan laid before God. "Job follows You because You have blessed him in every way, but if those things were taken away, it would be a different story. He would curse You."

In order to show the falsehood of Satan's argument—and to strengthen Job's faith at the same time—God allowed these multiple tragedies to crash into Job's life. The result? Job not only refused to curse God, he actually blessed Him. What a rebuke to the enemy! What a witness to the world.

It is a powerful testimony when a believer can praise God while suffering. Remember the story of Paul and Silas, arrested for preaching the gospel in the city of Philippi? The Bible tells us that the jailer had them stripped and flogged—a punishment so severe some people didn't even survive it. Then they were put in a dungeon, where their feet were fastened in stocks, which meant that their legs would have been as spread as far apart as humanly possible, causing excruciating pain.

So there they were in this hellhole, this dungeon, with their backs ripped open and their feet in stocks. And they hadn't done a thing to merit such terrible punishment! How did they respond? Here's what the Bible says: "But at midnight Paul and Silas were praying and singing hymns to God, and the prisoners were listening to them" (Acts 16:25).

That word "listened" could be translated *listened with great interest*. The prisoners were spellbound because they had never heard anybody sing praises to God in such a place. And that's about the time the Lord sent an earthquake. "At once all the prison doors flew open, and everybody's chains came loose. The jailer woke up, and when he saw the prison doors open, he drew his sword and was about to kill himself because he thought the prisoners had escaped. But Paul shouted, "Don't harm yourself! We are all here!"[22]

The Philippian jailer responded by saying, "Sirs, what must I do to be saved?" In effect he was saying, "I've been watching you guys. I've seen how you have taken such terrible punishment without cursing. I've seen how you can worship in the worst circumstances, and how you could have escaped but didn't. All I can say is, whatever you have, I want it."

Your circumstances may not be as dire as those of Paul and Silas. But never doubt that people are watching you. If you're in the midst of a hardship or difficulty, they're watching to see how you hold up—if you will really practice what you preach, and live out what you proclaim. The way you handle suffering in your life can bring great glory to God.

Paul the apostle also suffered from an unnamed "thorn in the flesh." No one really knows what it was, but he spoke of it in his letter to the Corinthian church, and said that he had asked the Lord on three separate occasions to remove it.

But God said no. Even though God had done miracles through Paul bringing healing to others, He chose not to bring that healing in the life of His loyal servant in this particular situation.

When Paul in essence asked, "Lord, why?" God gave him this answer: "My grace is all you need. My power works best in weakness" (2 Corinthians 12:9, NLT).

Was Paul discouraged by this answer, by God's refusal of his request? It sure doesn't sound like it! He goes on to say, "So now I am glad to boast about my weaknesses, so that the power of Christ can work through me. That's why I take pleasure in my weaknesses, and in the insults, hardships, persecutions, and troubles that I suffer for Christ. For when I am weak, then I am strong" (vv. 9-10).

So God can be glorified through your weakness. His light and power can shine through the chips and cracks in your life, using them to draw others to Himself.

#3 When God removes suffering

There is one more way God can be glorified through our suffering and hardships.

He can remove them. And sometimes that's just what He does. He doesn't always say "no," and He doesn't always say "wait." Sometimes He steps in immediately, bringing help, wisdom, comfort, and provision. I've seen that happen many, many times in my life and ministry.

On the other hand, He allowed His friend Lazarus to get sicker and die. But then the Lord raised him from the dead—so he could eventually die again!

Poor guy. He had to die twice. How bad is that? Once is bad enough.

But the point is, the Lord sometimes will allow calamity into the life of His child, and then bring glory to Himself by removing it.

The gospel of John tells the story of Jesus and His disciples encountering a man who had been blind from birth. The disciples asked their Master, "Why was this man born blind? Was it because of his own sins or his parents' sins?"[23] It sounds a little like a rehash of the accusations Job's counselors tossed out at him, doesn't it? "Whose fault was this? Why is he sick? Who committed this sin?" This is the same warped "word of faith" theology that says if you are sick, it's the result of your personal sin because (they allege) God never wants you sick. And if you'll just confess it, you will be healed. If you're not healed, it's because of your lack of faith.

It is Job's counselors revisited, and it is wrong counsel. Godly people can suffer too, and still be right in the middle of God's good plans and purposes.

Jesus had a strong answer for the disciples when they asked, "why was this man born blind? Was it because of his own sins or his parents' sins?"

"It was not because of his sins or his parents' sins," Jesus answered. "This happened so the power of God could be seen in him" (John 9:3, NLT).

God wanted to display His power by healing this man—as He did when He raised Lazarus from the dead. But we must also recognize that there are times when God will not heal the blind. He will not raise the dead. He will not do what we ask. And it is then that we must trust Him. It is then that we must do what Job did when his whole world fell apart. He said, "Praise the name of the Lord." He didn't say, "I understand this, I understand You." He simply said, "Lord, I trust You."

Job lived a real life in real time, and in the midst of his suffering, he couldn't read the end of his own story to see how things turned out. Yet he said, "Praise the name of the Lord."

We can ask God the "why" question anytime we want to. But I don't know if we're really going to be satisfied with His answers. If God came down to you on a shining cloud and explained His purposes to you, would it really make it any better? I don't know that it would.

As far as we know, Job was never given the "why" of all the tragedies that befell him. But He was given an incredible revelation of God's wisdom and power.

There was a time when Jesus asked, "God, why?" It was when He was in great agony, dying on the cross for your sins and my sins, and He cried out, "My God, My God, why have You forsaken Me?"

He did ask why. But notice that He prefaced it with, "My God, My God." It wasn't an accusation against the Father. Jesus was merely stating the reality of what was taking place in those awful hours, as all of the sin of the world was being placed upon Him who had known no sin. And as the Father turned His holy face away, the Son cried out, "Why have You forsaken Me?"

The fact is, Jesus was forsaken that I might be forgiven. But even in His great cry of grief and loneliness over His separation from the Father, as He bore the sins of the world for all time, Jesus still said, "*My* God, *My* God." There was complete trust in the Lord.

At this point you might be saying, "Well, I have a lot of questions for God. When I get to heaven I'm going to ask Him some things. In fact, I've got a list."

You just keep that list with you. Take it with you everywhere you go, and then if you die unexpectedly, you'll have it handy to pull out and ask God your questions when you stand before Him. I can just see you now:

> *"Lord, it's good to be here. Wow, look at that sea of glass and saphire throne. Look at all those angels. Very impressive. But listen... I've got this little list of questions I've been carrying around. It's here somewhere. Where did I put that—in my pocket? Where did my pockets go?"*

Somehow, I don't think that's the way it will be. I suggest to you that when you arrive in heaven, when you see your Creator, your God, your Savior in all His blazing glory, you'll forget all about your little list of questions. One commentator wrote, "I had a million questions to ask

God, but when I met Him, they all fled my mind and it didn't seem to matter."

Our perplexities, distressing as they may be, will one day be swept away.

Now we see things imperfectly as in a cloudy mirror, but then we will see everything with perfect clarity. All that I know now is partial and incomplete, but then I will know everything completely, just as God knows me now. (1 Corinthians 13:12, NLT)

Our sorrows and heartaches, heavy as they weigh on our souls, will one day be forgotten like a bad dream.

For the Lamb on the throne will be their Shepherd. He will lead them to the springs of life-giving water. And God will wipe every tear from their eyes. (Revelation 7:17, NLT)

#4 Suffering prepares us for the road ahead

Suffering can also be used by God to prepare us for a special task ahead of us. The Bible doesn't tell us what Job's task might have been after God completely restored him, but it certainly tells us what happened with Joseph in the book of Genesis.

Through unbelievable adversity as a young man, God prepared him for a task beyond his imagination. You remember his story: abandoned and betrayed by his brothers and sold into slavery, he was eventually elevated to a position of great power. As the Prime Minister of Egypt, the second most influential man in the world, he was given charge of Egypt's food stores during a worldwide famine.

Then the day came when ten of his brothers, who thought Joseph was long dead, came down to Egypt from Canaan to get food for their starving families. The moment Joseph saw and recognized them, he could have had them summarily executed on the spot.

Instead, he forgave them and made this amazing statement:

But as for you, you meant evil against me; but God meant it for good, in order to bring it about as it is this day, to save many people alive. (Genesis 50:20)

Earlier he had told them, "don't be angry with yourselves for selling me to this place. It was God who sent me here ahead of you to preserve your lives" (Genesis 45:5, NLT).

Did you catch that? Joseph didn't just say "God allowed it," though you could describe it that way, too. But he actually said, "God did it." Why? Joseph said, "To save many people alive."

God delivered Joseph from his brothers' jealousy, from a false accusation by his master's wife, and then from the dungeon so he could interpret the dream of the Pharaoh and make provision for the future. And many, many people—across that ancient world—lived as a result. The suffering he went through prepared him for the job that God had for him to do.

Maybe the Lord is allowing you to go through some difficult circumstances right now to prepare you for something He wants you to do tomorrow. I realize that thought might not comfort you all that much in your present distress.

You may be thinking, *No, this suffering doesn't make any sense at all. It's meaningless. There's no point to it.*

Joseph might have thought that same thing at several points in his life journey. It's certain that Job did! But the truth is, God might very well be preparing you to touch someone else's life in a way no one else could. If someone just found out they have cancer and you are a cancer survivor, you have no idea how much encouragement and perspective you can bring to such a person, who feels as though he or she has been handed a death sentence.

Or maybe a couple you know lost a child through illness or some terrible accident, and they are walking on the ragged edge of sanity, feeling like they can't go on another minute, much less another day. If you have lost a child in the past, and God has brought you healing, you can come along and say, "We lost a child too, and it was the hardest thing that ever happened to us. Though we still mourn that child, and though we're still dealing with it, and miss him every single day, we want you to know that God can help you each step of the way. His grace really will be sufficient for you." You have no idea how much comfort that can bring. And it would be something that only you could say. No one else could say those words with the same kind of credibility.

Recently we had a man named Brian Birdwell give his testimony at our church. Brian was in the Pentagon on September 11, 2001, when planes crashed into the World Trade Center and the Pentagon. Many of Brian's friends were killed that day. He survived, though he was burned over much of his body and had to go through multiple excruciating skin graft operations.

Afterwards I had lunch with Brian, and we had a lot of fun together. He is very witty and a great pleasure to be with. In my opinion, he is also a genuine American hero. Before we finished our meal, I asked him if he wanted to do something with me that afternoon. He thanked me, but then said, "Greg, I'd love to, but I can't. I have to go to a hospital."

"What's going on?" I asked him.

"Well," he said, "whenever I go speak in some location, I always find out where the local burn ward is, and I go and visit the patients."

I remember thinking how wonderful that was. Who could have a more effective ministry to burn victims than someone who had been through the agony of skin grafts and burn treatments, as Brian had? Imagine being an individual burned over most of your body, and thinking, *My life is over.* But then a survivor comes along and says, "Look. I know how hard it is. I have been there. But I got through it! And here is what God has been doing in and through my life since I got out of the hospital. He can do the same for you!"

Paul, who had his own serious issues with suffering, as we have said, wrote: "God is our merciful Father and the source of all comfort. He comforts us in all our troubles so that we can comfort others. When they are troubled, we will be able to give them the same comfort God has given us. For the more we suffer for Christ, the more God will shower us with his comfort through Christ." (2 Corinthians 1:3-5, NLT).

God will give you that comfort—over and beyond what you can personally contain—so that you can share it with others.

The Rest of the Story

In the final chapter of the book of Job, God restored everything to His righteous servant—double. He had passed the test, leaving an unforgettable example for us in the pages of Scripture. Though he could never replace the children he had lost, God gave him more, allowing him to enjoy his children and grandchildren.

Could it be that the hardships you find yourself facing today are preparing you for something just over the horizon—a ministry and a life beyond your imagination right now? I'll tell you this: God doesn't waste anything. Not one sorrow. Not one sigh. Not one tear.

Dr. Warren Wiersbe quotes a professor of history who said, "If Columbus had turned back, no one would have blamed him. But no one would have remembered him either." And Wiersbe concludes, "If you want to be memorable, sometimes you have to be miserable."

You might say, "Honestly, I don't see how I could handle one tenth of all the things Job faced. In fact, I can't handle suffering at all."

Don't worry. God knows what you can manage. He knows what you can take. And He will parcel it out accordingly. You just need to trust Him. God will give you what you need when you need it. Not before, never after, but just when it is needed. Until then, we must simply trust Him.

Corrie ten Boom, well-known author of *The Hiding Place*, was placed in a Nazi concentration camp along with her sister and her father. They were committed Christians, and their "crime" had been hiding Jewish people in their home, trying to protect them from Nazi genocide against all Jews in Hitler's Reich.

Both Corrie's father and sister died, and Corrie herself went through deep suffering during that time.

But she survived, and she spent the rest of her life traveling around the world as a self-described "tramp for the Lord," declaring that there was no pit so deep that God was not deeper still.

When Corrie was a little girl, she read a story about martyrs for the Christian faith, and was trying to process what these saints of God had endured for the sake of Christ. She said to her father, "Daddy, I am afraid that I will never be strong enough to be a martyr for Jesus Christ."

"Tell me," said that wise father, "when you take train trip to Amsterdam, when do I give you the money for the ticket? Three weeks before?"

"No, Daddy," she replied. "You give me the money for the ticket just before we get on the train."

"That's right," he replied. "And so it is with God's strength. Our Father in heaven knows when you will need the strength to be a martyr for Jesus Christ. He will supply all you need just in time."

As it turned out, God never required Corrie to die as a martyr, as her father and sister did. Even so, Corrie suffered much in her life, and God always gave her the strength she needed... just as her father had told her.

Hold Life Loosely

Here's something that hit me pretty hard as I studied Job's life: we need to hold everything God has given us loosely. We like to say, "*My* life, *my* marriage, *my* kids, *my* career, *my* 401k..." and on it goes.

But wait. Everything you have has come to you as a gift from God. Job found that out, and had to declare before God and man, "The Lord gives and the Lord takes away. Blessed be the name of the Lord."

Maybe you drive your new SUV through the car wash and admire the way it sparkles and gleams after you wipe it down. Don't forget that was given to you—it's a good gift from the Father.

Or you drive into the driveway of your home. Don't take it for granted! God has graced you and privileged you to live there.

You get up in the morning and feel like a million bucks, or finish a game of tennis and grab a nice long shower. Don't forget—your health and strength are a gift from God. You may be very careful to eat only organic stuff and exercise regularly, but God gave you your health. God has given you your life.

God has given you your wife. He has given you your husband. He has blessed you with children. He has given you everything. Hold it loosely. He may leave it in your hands for years; then again, he might take it tomorrow. That's up to Him to decide. But it all belongs to Him, and we should praise Him every day for what He has given us.

The truth is, everybody suffers. Calamity comes into every life—the righteous and the unrighteous, the godly and the ungodly. The good news is that the Lord can use suffering in the lives of His sons and daughters... to strengthen us spiritually... to make us more Christlike... to use us to minister to and comfort others... and to prepare us for future tasks that are completely off our personal charts.

But what about the unbeliever? What's his consolation? Where do the atheist and the agnostic go for comfort? What do they have to show for their pain, their tears, their bruises, and their calamities? Not much. It's just "hard luck," and then you die.

But what comfort we have in Christ! What an indescribable hope! He is worthy of our complete trust and confidence, no matter what we might be enduring at the moment.

Sometimes God can use sickness, tragedy, hardship, or difficulty to get our attention. The psalmist said, "Before I was afflicted I went astray, but now I keep your word.... It is good for me that I have been afflicted, that I may learn your statutes."[24]

Are you in a "hot place" right now? Do you find yourself in the fires of difficulty or crisis? You got bad news from the doctor. You were let go from your job. Your "significant other" dumped you. Maybe something else has happened that has rocked your world, and you don't know what to do.

You need to say, "God, help."

He has thousands of years of experience helping, comforting, and saving those who reach up to Him in faith.

‹THREE›

Cool in the Furnace

When the apostle Peter sat down to pen a letter to some churches that were facing persecution and trials, he had a word of counsel for them: "Don't let it surprise you."

He wrote: "Dear friends, don't be surprised at the fiery trials you are going through, as if something strange were happening to you. Instead, be very glad—because these trials will make you partners with Christ in his suffering, so that you will have the wonderful joy of seeing his glory when it is revealed to all the world" (1 Peter 4:12-13, NLT).

It's not unusual if you are being tempted or tested. It's not strange or bizarre if you find yourself going through the fire of trials. In spite of what you may have been taught, hardships and difficulties are a normal thing in the life of a committed follower of Jesus Christ.

We've just walked with Job through the fire, and then turned our attention to Joseph and the flames of testing he endured. But when you're talking about believers keeping their cool in a hot place, I don't know of any better story in Scripture than that of Shadrach, Meshach, and Abednego in the book of Daniel.

This is a Test...

It was Phillip Brooks who said, "Character may be manifested in the great moments, but it is made in the small ones."

Get used to the idea—there will be times in your life when your faith is tested, when you are challenged for what you believe. There will be multiple occasions when the temptation for you to go the wrong direction, say the wrong thing, or engage in the wrong activity will be very, very strong.

You might ask the question, "Will I be able to stand strong spiritually when this takes place?"

That's entirely up to you. The stand you make today will determine what kind of stand you will make tomorrow. So you have to think about it now, because you are laying the foundation for the years that remain ahead of you.

Shadrach, Meshach, and Abednego were young Israelite men who had been taken captive by the Babylonians and marched back to the capital of the evil empire.

The nation of Israel, home to Jerusalem and the Temple of the Lord, had been warned again and again about the coming calamities. The Lord spoke through prophet after prophet, describing the approaching judgment in terrifying detail—the judgment that was coming if His people continued in their idolatry, bloodshed, and sin, and refused to repent. But even though the Lord spoke to them in warnings both tender and stern, they closed their ears and would not turn back from their rebellion.

Through the prophet Isaiah, the Lord said:

*"All day long I have held out my hands
to an obstinate people,*

who walk in ways not good,
pursuing their own imaginations—
a people who continually provoke me
to my very face."
(Isaiah 65:2-3, NIV)

The Lord even specifically warned them how this judgment would come.

"Because you have not listened to me, I will gather
together all the armies of the north under King Nebu-
chadnezzar of Babylon, whom I have appointed as
my deputy. I will bring them all against this land and
its people and against the surrounding nations. I will
completely destroy you and make you an object of hor-
ror and contempt and a ruin forever. I will take away
your happy singing and laughter. The joyful voices of
bridegrooms and brides will no longer be heard. Your
millstones will fall silent, and the lights in your homes
will go out. This entire land will become a desolate
wasteland. Israel and her neighboring lands will serve
the king of Babylon for seventy years."
(Jeremiah 25:8-11, NLT)

How specific is that? God not only told them they would be conquered by another nation, He gave them the name of that nation and their king. And bear in mind that this prophecy was given years before the event actually took place, showing us once again the power and reliability of Scripture.

The prophets might as well have been preaching to a brick wall. The people of Judah were stuck on their false gods and simply would not listen. So the Lord said, in effect, "You want idols? I'll give you more idols than you can shake a stick at. Welcome to idol central—Babylon." And that is where they were taken, reaping what they had sown.

Before the powerful King Nebuchadnezzar struck the final blow against Jerusalem, flattening the walls and setting the city on fire, he invaded the city and marched back to Babylon with many of Israel's best and brightest young people. Among that group of captives were Daniel, Hananiah, Mishael, and Azariah—renamed by their captors Belteshazzar, Shadrach, Meshach, and Abednego.

Nebuchadnezzar's plan was to force these young men to abandon their faith and their culture to embrace the pagan ways and pagan gods of Babylon. Before the king accepted the captives into his service, he intended to erase every vestige of identification between these boys and their people and the God of their fathers.

How successful was he? Let's check it out in the first chapter of the book of Daniel.

During the third year of King Jehoiakim's reign in Judah, King Nebuchadnezzar of Babylon came to Jerusalem and besieged it. The Lord gave him victory over King Jehoiakim of Judah and permitted him to take some of the sacred objects from the Temple of God. So Nebuchadnezzar took them back to the land of Babylonia and placed them in the treasure-house of his god.

Then the king ordered Ashpenaz, his chief of staff, to bring to the palace some of the young men of Judah's royal family and other noble families, who had been brought to Babylon as captives. "Select only strong, healthy, and good-looking young men," he said. "Make sure they are well versed in every branch of learning,

*are gifted with knowledge and good judgment, and are
suited to serve in the royal palace. Train these young
men in the language and literature of Babylon." The
king assigned them a daily ration of food and wine
from his own kitchens. They were to be trained for
three years, and then they would enter the royal service.*

*Daniel, Hananiah, Mishael, and Azariah were four
of the young men chosen, all from the tribe of Judah.
The chief of staff renamed them with these Babylonian
names:*

*Daniel was called Belteshazzar.
Hananiah was called Shadrach.
Mishael was called Meshach.
Azariah was called Abednego.*

*But Daniel was determined not to defile himself by
eating the food and wine given to them by the king. He
asked the chief of staff for permission not to eat these
unacceptable foods.*
(vv. 1-8, NLT)

It is believed that these four young men were somewhere between fourteen and nineteen years old.

Think about that. Their world as they knew it changed
overnight. They had been torn away from their families
and friends, from their culture, and from the only home
they had ever known. After marching what must have
seemed like halfway around the world, they were thrust
into a bewildering world of paganism and unparalleled
luxury. As Jews, they would have been raised in relatively
simple conditions, eating simple foods, but now these

boys found themselves in the royal palace of the greatest superpower on earth.

What an experience that must have been for these Jewish kids! The Hanging Gardens of Babylon were one of the seven wonders of the ancient world. Some accounts speak of terraced gardens towering hundreds of feet into the air. Writing in 450 BC, the historian Herodotus said, "In addition to its size, Babylon surpasses in splendor any city in the known world." He went on to claim that the city's outer walls were 56 miles in length, 80 feet thick, and 320 feet high. Wide enough, he said, to allow a four-horse chariot to turn. Inside the walls were fortresses and temples with immense statues of solid gold. Rising above the city was the famous Tower of Babel, a temple to the god Marduk, that seemed to reach to the heavens.[25]

Living inside the royal palace meant living in jaw-dropping luxury, off the charts. And these teenage boys (always hungry, of course) were brought into the court of the king himself, with meals delivered directly from his kitchen. Culture shock? You'd better believe it. It must have left these young Hebrew boys stunned and disoriented.

Maybe you can identify a little with the major life changes they endured. Has your world changed lately? Perhaps something has happened in your life to move you from where you were to where you are now. Maybe you're new on a college campus. Maybe your business has required you to move to another part of the country. Maybe you are overseas serving our country in a place like Iraq or Afghanistan. Or maybe you've lost a spouse through death or divorce, and the world as you knew it has completely changed. You find yourself wondering how you will get through this time of transition.

That's how it was for these young Hebrews. But they weren't alone. The Lord was with them. Though Nebuchadnezzar had the power to change their location and change their names, he could not change their hearts. Even so, they were facing heavy temptation. It would have been easy for them to be seduced by all of this luxury. But because these boys had been raised right, they had the foundation to sustain them so they could effectively resist the enticements of the king.

The Foundations of Home

The staying power of these Hebrew youths has to be a tribute to a group of dads and moms back in Judah— perhaps slain by the Babylonians. And yet their work in parenting their children to love and serve God was bearing fruit even after they had left this earth.

It isn't easy to raise children to follow the ways of the Lord in this culture, either. We're living in a society that is largely hostile to our beliefs and values as Christians.

It wasn't always that way. Not so many years ago, you could turn on television and find primetime programs that actually supported the values of family. TV series like *Ozzie and Harriett, Leave It to Beaver*, and *Father Knows Best* reinforced the idea of family values and families sticking together.

How things have changed. The sitcoms on TV today mock the idea of traditional families and laugh at anything that upholds moral standards. And we're a long, long way from *Father Knows Best*. The dads on television today are oafs and buffoons who only care about sex, their expensive toys, and an unending supply of beer. The idea of any-thing even approaching an intact family is almost a freak-ish thing to many people today. Now, in the way these sitcoms are written, "Kids Know Best" and "Father Is an Idiot!"

And of course we are reaping the results of those atti-tudes in our culture. It's hard, because as parents we want our children to embrace the truth we raised them with.

As a mom or dad, I'm sure your normal prayer for your son or your daughter would be something like this: "Lord, keep them safe today, help them, and guide their steps." But what we really ought to be praying as moms and dads is, "Lord, bring them to Yourself and glorify Yourself through their lives."

Here's why. Your kids don't belong to you. My kids don't belong to me. Oh, I know we call them "My son, my daughter, my grandchild," or whatever. But in reality, they belong to the Lord. They are on loan to us from God. Our job is to commit them to the Lord, point them in the right direction, and then pray that they would know the Lord and that God would be glorified through their lives.

If you had been the mother of Shadrach, Meshach, and Abednego, you would never have prayed that they would be taken captive into Babylon and into the service of this bloodthirsty king. As a godly parent, you would be very concerned about a situation like that because you wouldn't want your boys to abandon their faith and get swallowed up in pagan culture.

And you certainly would never have prayed, "Lord, I'm hoping that before they get out of their teens, they'll end up in a fiery furnace." But the Lord had a plan for these young men—a plan that included testing, defiance of the established order, and deadly danger. But in the process, He would gain great glory through their lives. And here we are, some 2,500 years later, still telling the story of their courageous choices.

Had you been the mother of Daniel, you would never have prayed, "O Lord, let Israel be taken captive and let my son one day be put into a den of hungry lions." No loving parent would pray such a thing. And yet the Lord allowed it, and look how He was glorified through the life of Daniel.

Had you been Mary, you never would have prayed, "Lord, I hope my Son will one day be falsely accused, stripped, beaten, and crucified between two thieves." Could anything be more heartbreaking than that? Nothing is harder for a parent than to see their child suffer. Could she ever imagine that those once tiny hands of her little boy would have spikes driven through them? In her worst nightmare, could she have foreseen that the forehead she used to kiss would be torn and bloodied by a crown of thorns? Could she have visualized that young man who had been her pride and joy so beaten and bludgeoned that his face was beyond recognition?

If you were His mother and saw such things, you would have to cry out in your heart, "This is the worst thing that could possibly happen!" And yet through His sacrifice, through His death and resurrection, He would become the salvation of the whole world—including hers!

As dads and moms who love the Lord, then, we need to pray that God will gain great glory through our sons' and daughters' lives. Yes, Lord, please protect them. Please bless them, guide them, and keep Your hand on them.

But use them for Your glory.

A Matter of Conscience

If you were the most powerful man in the whole world, it follows that you would have the best cuisine in the world. How would you like to be the chef that served Nebuchadnezzar a burned dinner roll, cold potatoes, or lumpy gravy? It would probably be the last meal you would ever cook on the planet. So you can be pretty sure the person on top of the food chain—the king—got the best of the best.

And now these Hebrew teenagers had access to the king's table. I'm sure that would have meant the finest wines, all of the latest culinary treats, and the most exotic spices available.

So here was the greatest food—literally on the face of the earth—available to him, and yet Daniel decides this is a time to stand on principle. Daniel 1:8 tells us, "Daniel was determined not to defile himself by eating the food and wine given to them by the king."

How would Daniel have been defiling himself by eating delicious food from this five-star kitchen? Some of it may have been forbidden by Mosaic law, but I think the primary reason he shunned the food was because it had been offered to an idol, a false god.

As I mentioned, Babylon was idol central, with a pantheon of gods and goddesses. So no doubt this food coming from the king's kitchen would have been dedicated to Nebuchadnezzar's god. For Daniel, it was a compromise. In his heart, he didn't feel right about it.

Sometimes there are things we will simply choose to refrain from doing as a believer because we feel uneasy about it. There's a sense that it's not right before God, and while we don't condemn anyone else for doing what we choose not to do, it just feels better that way in our heart of hearts.

In the book of Romans, Paul writes: "Whatsoever is not of faith is sin." Or as another translation puts it, "Anyone who believes that something he wants to do is wrong shouldn't do it. He sins if he does, for he thinks it is wrong, and so for him it is wrong. Anything that is done apart from what he feels is right is sin."[26]

For Daniel, eating the king's food was wrong.

Is there something in your life that you are doing that would be similar to this? Something you have rationalized, but yet, in your heart of hearts, you know isn't right? If so, you should take the same stand that Daniel and his friends took.

We might look at this and say, "Well, why was it such a big deal? Was it worth drawing a line in the sand at that point and possibly losing his life?" Daniel chose to make a stand in this relatively small area of his life... and it was a big deal to him. As we will see later, standing firm in little things prepared him for even greater tests in the years to come.

The issue was bigger than simply missing out on some great meals. Having access to the king's table was also a huge point for your résumé—something like climbing the corporate ladder of Babylon. As a young man, Daniel had this sort of unparalleled access just fall into his lap, and he was willing to turn away from it.

Daniel's Determined Purpose

There is always a temptation to compromise if you know it might help you accomplish some desirable objectives. *If you cheat on that résumé, you'll probably get the job. Or if you lie about yourself, people will like you more. Or if you cut corners on this job site, you'll see the building go up more quickly and it will be better for everyone.* But if you do these things, if you make these compromises, it will come back to bite you later. Perhaps even worse. Scripture warns that you will reap what you sow.

The King James Version of the Bible says, "But Daniel purposed in his heart that he would not defile himself..." I don't think you can improve on that wording. Deep down in his inner man, Daniel resolved to be true to his convictions before God no matter what.

We need more people today with that kind of purpose, resolve, and courage. The apostle Paul said, "For my determined purpose is that I may know Him that I may progressively become more deeply and intimately acquainted with Him."[27]

What is your determined purpose in life? Everyone has some kind of purpose. On another occasion, Paul wrote to Timothy, "But you, Timothy, certainly know what I teach, and how I live, and what my purpose in life is."[28]

If someone were to ask you what your purpose in life is, what would you say?

My purpose in life is to have fun.
My purpose in life is to experience pleasure.
My purpose in life is to be successful.
My purpose in life is to get to the top of my profession.
My purpose in life is to make money.
My purpose in life is to be happy.

What you should be seeking is not happiness, but holiness. Not pleasure, but purpose. Not success, but significance.

Because he knew his purpose, Daniel struck a deal with the chief official in charge of the king's food program.

But Daniel determined that he would not defile himself by eating the king's food or drinking his wine, so he asked the head of the palace staff to exempt him from the royal diet. The head of the palace staff, by God's grace, liked Daniel, but he warned him, "I'm afraid of what my master the king will do. He is the one who assigned this diet and if he sees that you are not as healthy as the rest, he'll have my head!"
(Daniel 1:8-10, The Message)

You can understand why this Babylonian official had sweaty palms over this deal. If word got back to Nebuchadnezzar that several of his prime "foreign exchange" students weren't eating right, the official wouldn't only be relieved of his duties, he would be relieved of his head.

But Daniel, who was firm but courteous, persuaded the man to give the experiment a test.

"Test us for ten days on a diet of vegetables and water,"
Daniel said. "At the end of the ten days, see how we look compared to the other young men who are eating the king's food. Then make your decision in light of what you see." So the attendant agreed to Daniel's suggestion and tested them for ten days.
(Daniel 1:12-14, NLT)

Daniel turned down a rich diet to maintain a rich relationship with the Lord. This story reminds us that a little with God is better than a lot without Him.

As believers, we say no to some lifestyle choices that maybe we'd like to say yes to now and then. We make decisions in life about what we will do with our time, how we will spend our resources, what we will allow to fill our thoughts, and what goals we will reach for as we head into our future.

There are those who choose to live in the way of the world, and those who choose to live in the way of the Lord. There are those who climb aboard the merry-go-round of selfishness, partying, drinking, and anything else this world has to offer. And then there are those of us who get on that straight and narrow path that leads to life.

All I would say is that you go ahead and get on your road, and I'll get on mine. Then, at the end of our life's journey, let's compare notes and see who made the best choice. I am confident already that I have made the right choice. And whatever I have given up, God has made it up to me a thousand times over.

Remember what Scripture says about the choice Moses made as a young man? "By faith Moses, when he had grown up, refused to be known as the son of Pharaoh's daughter. He chose to be mistreated along with the people of God rather than to enjoy the pleasures of sin for a short time. He regarded disgrace for the sake of Christ as of greater value than the treasures of Egypt, because he was looking ahead to his reward."[29]

We sometimes forget how much Moses gave up to identify with his own people. He had been raised in the court of the Pharaoh. According to the ancient Jewish historian Josephus, he was being groomed to be the next Pharaoh of Egypt. That meant that Moses would have had unparalleled wealth and power—virtually anything he wanted in life—and yet he simply turned his back on it to stand with his enslaved and persecuted people. He felt that the worst prospects of walking with God were better than the best the world could ever offer.

Shadrach, Meshach, Abednego, and Daniel made this stand, and God honored that step of faith. They came through the ten-day diet looking healthier than everybody else. In fact, the Lord not only honored these young men with vibrant health, He gave them wisdom far beyond their contemporaries. If they had put it in book form, I'm sure it would have been a hit on the New York Times bestseller list: *Get Fit, Look Good, and Get Closer to God in 10 Days.*

To these four young men God gave knowledge and understanding of all kinds of literature and learning. And Daniel could understand visions and dreams of all kinds.

> *At the end of the time set by the king to bring them in, the chief official presented them to Nebuchadnezzar. The king talked with them, and he found none equal to Daniel, Hananiah, Mishael and Azariah; so they entered the king's service. In every matter of wisdom and understanding about which the king questioned them, he found them ten times better than all the magicians and enchanters in his whole kingdom. (Daniel 1:17-20, NIV)*

Nebuchadnezzar was blown away by the maturity and insights these godly young men possessed. But it was Daniel's ability to interpret dreams that would bring him to national prominence beyond what anyone could have imagined.

The King and the Dream

If God gives us unusual talents or abilities in a particular area of our lives, then it follows that He plans on using that gifting for His purposes. We just have to make sure we stay available to Him—a clean, ready, yielded life, ready to roll when He says, "Let's roll."

It all started with the king's bad dream. If you and I have a bad dream, we shake it off and maybe chalk it up to the cold pizza we ate before we got into bed. But when the ruler of the Babylonian empire had a bad dream, it became a national crisis.

Here's what Scripture says:

One night during the second year of his reign, Nebu-chadnezzar had such disturbing dreams that he couldn't sleep. He called in his magicians, enchanters, sorcerers, and astrologers, and he demanded that they tell him what he had dreamed. As they stood before the king, he said, "I have had a dream that troubles me, and I must know what it means."

Then the astrologers answered the king in Aramaic, "Long live the king! Tell us the dream, and we will tell you what it means."
(Daniel 2:1-4, NLT)

When Nebuchadnezzar called in all the royal astrologers and soothsayers, he wanted immediate satisfaction. After all, it was their job to understand and interpret messages from the spiritual world. I have an idea these guys did pretty well for themselves. A cushy job in the palace, sitting out under the stars every night, health care... you name it. So now, as far as the king was concerned, it was time for them to deliver the goods.

But they couldn't. They couldn't tell the king what he had dreamed, and they were in deep trouble.

Then the astrologers... said to the king, "Sir, tell us the dream and then we can tell you what it means."

But the king replied, "I tell you, the dream is gone—I can't remember it. And if you won't tell me what it was and what it means, I'll have you torn limb from limb and your houses made into heaps of rubble! But I will give you many wonderful gifts and honors if you tell me what the dream was and what it means. So, begin!"

They said again, "How can we tell you what the dream means unless you tell us what it was?"

The king retorted, "I can see your trick! You're trying to stall for time until the calamity befalls me that the dream foretells. But if you don't tell me the dream, you certainly can't expect me to believe your interpretation!"

The astrologers replied to the king, "There isn't a man alive who can tell others what they have dreamed! And there isn't a king in all the world who would ask such a thing! This is an impossible thing the king requires. No one except the gods can tell you your dream, and they are not here to help."

Upon hearing this, the king was furious, and sent out orders to execute all the wise men of Babylon. And Daniel and his companions were rounded up with the others to be killed. (Daniel 2:4-13, TLB)

Even though it is evident that Daniel, Shadrach, Meshach, and Abednego had not been part of the meeting with the astrologers, they were to be put to death along with all the others. So when the decree went out, it caught Daniel and his friends flatfooted.

> *When Arioch, the commander of the king's guard, had gone out to put to death the wise men of Babylon, Daniel spoke to him with wisdom and tact. He asked the king's officer, "Why did the king issue such a harsh decree?" Arioch then explained the matter to Daniel. At this, Daniel went in to the king and asked for time, so that he might interpret the dream for him. (Daniel 2:14-16, NIV)*

So Daniel did exactly what I imagine you and I would have done. He went home, grabbed his best friends, and said, "C'mon guys. Let's hit our knees. We need to put this in the Lord's hands." He prayed with Shadrach, Meshach, and Abednego, and God heard their prayer, revealing the secret to Daniel. Armed with the confidence that God had really spoken to him, Daniel went back to stand before the king.

To paraphrase, he said to Nebuchadnezzar. "Okay, here's what you dreamt last night. You saw a giant image. Am I right? Head of gold, breast and arms of silver, belly and thighs of brass, and feet of iron and clay."

Daniel was basically giving Nebuchadnezzar a picture of the world to come, and the kingdoms that would be in the ascendancy. Babylon was the head of gold. The breast and arms of silver would be the Medo-Persian Empire that would overthrow Babylon. And he took it right up to ancient Rome, the revival of Rome, and the return of Christ—which is yet to come. Unbelievable. What a sweeping vision this Babylonian ruler had experienced! But it took a servant of the living God to put it into perspective.

Nebuchadnezzar was impressed, to put it mildly.

Then King Nebuchadnezzar fell prostrate before Daniel and paid him honor and ordered that an offering and incense be presented to him. The king said to Daniel, "Surely your God is the God of gods and the Lord of kings and a revealer of mysteries, for you were able to reveal this mystery." (Daniel 2:46-47, NIV)

This may have been the only time in the king's whole life when he fell prostrate before anyone. He acknowledged Daniel's God to be "the God of gods and the Lord of kings."

You would have thought right there on the spot Nebuchadnezzar would have believed in the Lord. Not on your life. Just a few verses later, we find the king erecting a ninety-foot, solid-gold statue—probably of himself. In the dream, just the head was gold. But in real life, Nebuchadnezzar made the whole image gold. And then he took it a step further, saying, "Command everybody in Babylon to bow down before this image. And if you don't, you will be put to death."

It was the number one show in Babylon. In fact, it was the only show in Babylon. Wherever you were, whatever you were doing, when you heard the band crank up the Babylonian Idol theme song, you were supposed to bow before the image.

Let's just say it was politically incorrect not to bow down before that image. In fact, if you didn't bow, you would burn. Literally. The king had a huge furnace blazing, ready for the first person who didn't cooperate with the program.

Needless to say, everyone cooperated.

Everyone but Shadrach, Meshach, and Abednego.

No Room for Compromise

It was easy enough to spot these three Israeli teenagers. They were the only people standing up while the rest of the empire bowed down.

Why didn't they bow? It goes back to the beginning of this chapter. If these young men refused to compromise in something as small as not eating foods that had been offered to idols, then they certainly weren't going to bow to a ninety-foot graven image.

In reality, there was no room for compromise here. These three guys knew God's Word, and God had told them in Exodus 20, "You shall have no other gods before Me. You shall not make for yourself a carved image—any likeness of anything that is in heaven above, or that is in the earth beneath, or that is in the water under the earth; you shall not bow down to them nor serve them. For I, the LORD your God, am a jealous God (vv. 3-5).

How clear is that? Worshipping Nebuchadnezzar's statue would be an act of blatant adultery, and there was no way these three godly Hebrews were going to do it.

But here's an interesting thought. The story tells us everybody bowed. And yet we know that there were thousands and thousands of Israelites in Babylonian captivity who were also supposedly believers in the same Lord God of Shadrach, Meshach, and Abednego. So I think we can safely assume that there were many believers who were compromising and bowing along with everyone else.

Before you condemn them, think how hard this would be. Talk about peer pressure! Everyone in the whole nation is bowing... except you. It would be so very easy to just fall in line and say in your heart, *Well, God knows I don't really worship this thing. It's just a hunk of metal, not the real God.*

Let's face it, no one likes to stand out, or to be thought of as a freak or a fanatic. The herding instinct is very strong in human beings. Maybe that's why the Bible compares us to sheep.

Sheepish Believers

Scripture says of the Lord, "He will feed His flock like a shepherd; He will gather the lambs with His arm."[30] We love that picture. It's poetic. It's picturesque. It's pretty. Jesus said, "My sheep hear My voice, and I know them, and they follow Me."[31] We like that idea, too.

But here's one we don't like so well:

All we like sheep have gone astray;
We have turned, every one, to his own way;
(Isaiah 53:6)

Sheep are an almost completely defenseless animal. They don't run very quickly or have strong claws or teeth, which makes them completely dependent upon the shepherd. They also happen to be one of the dumbest animals on the face of the earth, because they have a tendency to get together and do whatever the other sheep are doing.

I read an article in the newspaper about something that happened in Istanbul. It seems that hundreds of sheep simply jumped off a cliff. The first one got it into his wooly little brain to jump to his death, and then, as the shepherds watched in stunned amazement, fifteen hundred others followed!

Now that is really insane. And yet there is a reason why God so often compares us to these mentally-challenged animals. We're so like them! We want to fit in.

We want to be cool. We want to be accepted by everybody else. We don't want to be the odd man (or woman) out.

That's what makes this story about Shadrach, Meshach, and Abednego so inspiring. There were thousands upon thousands of people who were upright one moment and falling down to worship a golden statue the next.

All but three Hebrew boys, who wouldn't do it. (Daniel isn't mentioned in this passage, but I can't imagine him bowing either.) The king, of course, finds out about it and calls Shadrach, Meshach, and Abednego into his presence. He wants to have words with them.

> *Nebuchadnezzar said to them, "Is it true, Shadrach, Meshach, and Abednego, that you refuse to serve my gods or to worship the gold statue I have set up? I will give you one more chance to bow down and worship the statue I have made when you hear the sound of the musical instruments. But if you refuse, you will be thrown immediately into the blazing furnace. And then what god will be able to rescue you from my power? (Daniel 3:14-15, NLT)*

Those last words, of course, were a direct challenge to the God of Israel. It's ironic, because just a little bit earlier, Nebuchadnezzar had called the God of Daniel the God of kings. And now he says, "What god will get you out of this mess? Oh, you may have a God that can tell dreams and interpret them, but this is a whole different matter. Your God won't get you out of this."

> *Shadrach, Meshach, and Abed-Nego answered and said to the king, "O Nebuchadnezzar, we have no need to answer you in this matter. If that is the case, our God whom we serve is able to deliver us from the*

burning fiery furnace, and He will deliver us from your hand, O king. But if not, let it be known to you, O king, that we do not serve your gods, nor will we worship the gold image which you have set up."
(Daniel 3:16-18)

I love these guys! "We're not going to do it. It's not going to happen. If God spares us, great. We don't want to die, but if God chooses not to spare us and we perish in those flames, then so be it. But we are not going to worship your god, and we are not going to bow before that image."

The Key to Their Courage

Every Christian will have to make his or her stand sooner or later. In some way, shape, or form, you are going to be asked to bow before some god. Before some principle. Before some idea. You will be asked to keep your convictions to yourself, get into line, and do what everyone else does. What will you do? Will you stand up for your faith and face the consequences, or will you cave in and take the path of least resistance?

Shadrach, Meshach, and Abednego chose to make their stand. And they were in really big trouble. Nebuchadnezzar, of course, was used to having everything go his way. He'd read his own press clippings, and his heart was filled with pride. When three mere teenagers defied him in front of everyone, he went volcanic.

That's the way it can be. People can get angry at you when you stand up for your convictions. But you just hold your course.

From the pages of church history, we read the story

of a Christian who was brought before a Roman emperor and told he must renounce his faith. The emperor said to him, "Give up Christ or I will banish you."

The Christian said, "You can't banish me from Christ, for God says, 'I will never leave you or forsake you.'"

The ruler said, "I will confiscate your property."

The Christian replied, "My treasures are laid up in heaven. You can't touch them."

The emperor then said, "I will kill you."

The Christian replied, "I have been dead to the world in Christ for forty years. My life is hid with Christ in God. You can't touch it."

The emperor then turned to the members of his court and said in disgust, "What can you do with such a fanatic?"

What can you do? Pray that we will have many more believers in this nation just like him—people like Shadrach, Meshach, and Abednego, who will stand up for what is right no matter what the cost.

Let's pick up the story again in Daniel chapter 3.

Then Nebuchadnezzar was full of fury, and the expression on his face changed toward Shadrach, Meshach, and Abed-Nego. He spoke and commanded that they heat the furnace seven times more than it was usually heated. And he commanded certain mighty men of valor who were in his army to bind Shadrach, Meshach, and Abed-Nego, and cast them into the burning fiery furnace. Then these men were bound in their coats, their trousers, their turbans, and their other garments, and were cast into the midst of the burning fiery furnace. Therefore, because the king's command was urgent, and the furnace exceedingly hot, the flame

*of the fire killed those men who took up Shadrach,
Meshach, and Abed-Nego. And these three men, Shadrach, Meshach, and Abed-Nego, fell down bound into
the midst of the burning fiery furnace.*

*Then King Nebuchadnezzar was astonished; and he
rose in haste and spoke, saying to his counselors, "Did
we not cast three men bound into the midst of the
fire?"*

They answered and said to the king, "True, O king."

*"Look!" he answered, "I see four men loose, walking
in the midst of the fire; and they are not hurt, and the
form of the fourth is like the Son of God." (vv. 19-25)*

You might ask yourself, "What would I have done?
Would I have bowed? Would I have defied the powerful king? Could I take a stand like these three guys?" You
will determine that by the decisions you make today. You
may never face a test as dramatic as the one we just read
about, but tests will come. Temptations will come. And
many of those moments of great testing will come when
you are alone, when no one is looking.

We're foolish if we think we can stand up to temptation—the lure of the world, our own flesh, and the devil—
in our own strength and wisdom. We need help from on
high.

The key to the courage and serenity of these men in
the midst of those flames was their Companion! Nebuchadnezzar said it best: "The fourth looks like the Son of
God."

Now, in fairness, this passage could also be translated,
"The son of the gods." I don't know that Nebuchadnezzar
necessarily realized that the fourth person in the flames

was Jesus Christ. I don't know what he thought. All he knew was that he tossed three men in a blazing furnace, and they were walking around in the fire like it was a Sunday stroll in the park.

And Someone Else was walking with them.

Just that quickly, the king didn't want to mess with these guys anymore. He had great respect—not necessarily belief at that point, but yet respect for the God they represented.

Are you in a fiery trial right now? Are you in the hot waters of temptation? Know this. You are not alone in life.

Jesus is there with you each step of the way. The Lord says:

> *When you pass through the waters, I will be with you;*
> *And through the rivers, they shall not overflow you.*
> *When you walk through the fire, you shall not be*
> *burned,*
> *Nor shall the flame scorch you.*
> *(Isaiah 43:2)*

Jesus said, "Surely I am with you always, to the very end of the age."

And again, "I will never leave you nor forsake you."[32]

Take your stand for the Lord, in things great and small, and even though you may feel the heat, your Companion will never leave your side.

‹FOUR›

In the Company of Lions

A number of years ago, several of us from the church took a trip to Africa to visit a missions hospital. Since we had a day or two of free time, we went on a guided game drive out into the bush to see some of the animals.

I'd seen pictures of giraffes and zebras since I was old enough to open a picture book, and I'd seen them live in the zoo, of course, but it was still exciting to see them up close, running around on their own turf. Off in the distance we saw a rhino, and we all wondered what it would be like if he decided to go one on one with our truck. But the highlight of that excursion was a pride of lions.

We got very close to them. As long as you remain in your vehicle, our guide told us, the lions won't bother you. But if you decided to get out and take a stroll among them, they would immediately attack.

One man in the truck with us was more than a little drunk, and he wanted to get out and "see the lions." He kept trying to open the little gate on our truck to get out.

The man in charge said, "Sir, you can't see the lions."

"But I want to see the lions." I can tell you that if the lions had eaten this guy, they would have been drunk for a week.

These are ferocious creatures. And if they choose to kill you, it's all over. So you don't want to mess with lions.

The well-loved story from Daniel chapter six isn't so much a story of Daniel in the lion's den as it of the lions in Daniel's den. Because the hand of Almighty God was upon him. This isn't just the story of a man who survived a night with ferocious animals, it's the story of a God who stands with His sons and daughters when they face any kind of adversity or hardship.

A Den of Our Own

In this little book, we've considered a good man named Job, who faced a fiery trial beyond what most of us could imagine. We've also encountered Daniel and his three close friends, Shadrach, Meshach, and Abednego, who made up their minds not to defile themselves with the king's food, no matter what. Building on that foundation of faith and commitment, the three friends of Daniel refused to bow to the king's idol, though they faced execution by burning.

Each of these accounts from Scripture tells a unique story of perseverance, courage, faith, and the faithfulness of God. Unique, and yet not unusual. Every one of us will have a day like Job's, when the bottom suddenly falls out of our world. In our own time and in our own way, we're all going to face fiery furnaces or lion's dens.

Jesus told His disciples, "I have told you all this so that you may have peace in me. Here on earth you will have many trials and sorrows. But take heart, because I have overcome the world."[33]

As much as we might like to think so, you and I are not exempt from those "many trials and sorrows." Now, if we were in charge of life, we would probably never face any hardship. If we were able to chart out each day and could fill in all the blanks, I'm sure our choices would be ones that would personally benefit us. "Today _____ will happen to me."

We would never fill in the blank with "I will get sick" or "I'll get a flat tire on my way to work." No, we would write things like, "I will have a perfect day with blue skies and green lights" and things along those lines. And yet it is often through the difficult circumstances—painful and perplexing though they may be—that we learn some of the greatest and most enduring lessons of life.

It was that way in the life of Daniel. If you're in a "hot place" of some kind right now, take heart! Through this amazing Bible account, we're going to learn how Daniel was able to face the worst of circumstances. He not only came through this trial with flying colors, in the process he brought glory and honor to the name of his God.

And you can't get any better than that.

A New King, A New Challenge

Daniel chapter five gives us the dramatic conclusion of the mighty Babylonian empire. Nebuchadnezzar had died. His grandson Belshazzar, who openly defied and mocked God, had been weighed in God's balances and found lacking. And on the very night he was given that pronouncement of judgment, he was slain in a surprise attack by the Medes and the Persians. Stepping into that empty throne, Darius the Mede took over the empire.

Daniel at this time was in his mid-nineties, a man who radiated goodness and integrity. Recognizing a good man when he saw one, Darius promoted Daniel, intending to place him over the whole kingdom. And that set off a chain of events that eventually landed this godly prophet and leader in a den of hungry lions.

> Darius the Mede decided to divide the kingdom into
> 120 provinces, and he appointed a high officer to
> rule over each province. The king also chose Daniel
> and two others as administrators to supervise the
> high officers and protect the king's interests. Daniel
> soon proved himself more capable than all the other
> administrators and princes. Because of his great abil-
> ity, the king made plans to place him over the entire
> empire. Then the other administrators and princes
> began searching for some fault in the way Daniel was
> handling his affairs, but they couldn't find anything
> to criticize. He was faithful and honest and always
> responsible. (Daniel 6:1-5, NLT)

So what were the reasons for this man's remarkable
conduct? What set him apart? Why is he remembered in
Hebrews 11, the hall of faith chapter? Why do we celebrate him today as one of the heroes of the faith? As we
wrap up this little study on *Why, God?*, I'd like to point
out three enduring foundation stones of this man's life.

Daniel Was a Spiritual Man

Scripture says, "Because of his great ability, the king made
plans to place him over the entire empire." But the King
James Version translates it, "Because an excellent spirit
was in him." Or, to say it another way, "Because spirit pre-
dominated." For Daniel, the spiritual life wasn't merely an
afterthought or something he did when he found time in
his busy schedule. He was a man whose very life revolved
around his commitment to God; it permeated everything
he said and did.

Sometimes when we hear that a person is "spiritual," we think of him or her as being out of touch, not living in the real world, or (how shall I say it?) weird. But nothing could be further from the truth, because the truly spiritual man or woman will be a very practical person as well.

In the Amplified Bible, 2 Timothy 1:7 tells us, "For God did not give us a spirit of timidity (of cowardice, of craven and cringing and fawning fear), but [He has given us a spirit] of power and of love and of calm and well-balanced mind and discipline and self-control." A Spirit-filled believer will live a life that honors and glorifies God. Ephesians 5 tells us, "Be filled with the Spirit. Speak to one another with psalms, hymns and spiritual songs. Sing and make music in your heart to the Lord" (vv. 18-19, NIV).

When we think about being filled with the Spirit, we might imagine some wild emotional experience. But although being filled with the Spirit can and sometimes will include emotions, it won't necessarily always be that way.

What exactly did the apostle Paul mean when he used the term "filled"? One translation of the word pictures a steady wind filling the sails of a ship. So the idea is that the wind of God wants to fill the sails of your ship as you are moving along the sea of life. In another place in Scripture, the same word is translated *permeated,* picturing the truth that God wants to soak and saturate everything that we say or think or do.

To be filled with the Spirit means that the Holy Spirit is a part of all that you're involved in. He's a part of your prayer life. He's a part of your worship life. He's a part of your business life. He's a part of your vacation. He's a part of everything that touches your life in any way. That is what it is to be a Spirit-filled and Spirit-led believer.

Is this some big one-time experience, never to be repeated? No, because the original language implies this is something you should be receiving over and over and over again. Be continually filled with the Spirit.

Let's say you went out and bought yourself a brand new car. You drove it around town for a few days, and really liked the way it performed for you. But suddenly it started sputtering, and not running as well as it had in the beginning. Finally, it just chugged to a stop and wouldn't go any further. "What's the problem here?" you ask. "I just bought this car. I don't even have a couple of hundred miles on it yet."

You have that stalled-out new car towed back to the dealer, demanding an explanation. "Hmm," he says, slipping the key into the ignition and trying to start it a couple of times. "Umm... sir... do you see this little light on your fuel gauge? Some people call that an idiot light. It means you're out of gas. You need to fill your car up with gas every now and then."

"Oh," you say. "I never thought of that."

"Yes, sir. You see, you've got to keep refilling your car over and over if you want to keep going."

The same is true in life. You're cruising along, enjoying life and the scenery, experiencing peace and success in your family, your marriage, your business, and your ministry. Suddenly, however, problem after problem start cropping up, and life suddenly doesn't seem to be working very well.

Maybe you need a refill. Maybe you need to say, "Lord, give me the power of Your Holy Spirit to be a better husband. Give me the power of the Holy Spirit to be a better father. To be a better witness. To be a better worker. To be a better whatever You have called me to be."

So let the Holy Spirit fill your sails. Let the Holy Spirit permeate your life. Be filled with the Holy Spirit again and again and again.

Daniel was a man who was spiritual. That stands out in this story. And I might also add that this was a man who was living a spiritual life in a very unspiritual place—Babylon. "Idol Central," as I mentioned earlier. It was a place of perverted religion, immorality, and cruelty. Yet there was Daniel, in the midst of it all, living in a house somewhere near the palace. Despite all those allurements, temptations, and enticements, he remained righteous... and even grew stronger and stronger in spirit.

Sometimes we think the way to stay strong in the Lord is to always be surrounded by Christians. There's some truth in that. It's important that we go out of our way to spend time in fellowship with our Christian brothers and sisters. But that doesn't mean enveloping ourselves in some kind of Christian bubble, separating ourselves completely from every contact with the world. Some of us want to put our kids in Christian schools, work in a Christian workplace, and only patronize Christian-owned businesses.

I can appreciate the desire to surround yourself—as much as possible—with believers all day. But not all of us have that luxury. In fact, you may find yourself today in a very godless environment, surrounded by people who scoff at Christian values and have no regard at all for the things of the Lord. You may be wondering, *Can I survive spiritually in this place?*

The answer is yes. If Daniel could, then you can. Daniel was able to not only survive but to flourish.

When you find yourself surrounded by nonbelievers, you have two choices. The easy choice is to simply blend into the woodwork, making yourself and your beliefs invisible. Doing your best not to rock the boat or arouse any hostility, however, might mean that you are compromising your convictions and beliefs. That's one option.

The other option is to stand up and be counted.

I heard the story of some problems fish processors were having in shipping codfish from the East Coast to the West Coast. When it arrived, it was spoiled. So they tried freezing it. But when it arrived it was mushy to the taste. So they tried to send it live, but when it arrived it was dead.

Then someone came up with the bright idea to put the mortal enemy of the codfish—the catfish—in the crate when it was shipped. So that's what they did, and when the cod arrived they were alive and well, because they had been running from the catfish the whole time. And people who ate those harried codfish said it was the best they had ever tasted.

So what's the point? Maybe God has put catfish in your tank to keep your spirit alive and well. You know who I'm talking about. It's that one person who always seems to be hassling you, needling you, or trying to bring you down with negative comments. It might even be your brother or sister... or mom or dad. It might be the person who sits next to you in school or works next to you on the worksite or has the cubicle next to you at your office. Or maybe it's the neighbor right next door.

That's your catfish. That's your "irregular person," as one Christian author put it. And that is also the unlikely person God can use to make you stronger in spirit.

Daniel Was a Man of Purpose and Personal Integrity

The Bible says, "he was faithful, always responsible, and completely trustworthy."[34] What a great compliment. Could that be said of you?

I believe this stellar résumé dates back to Daniel chapter one, where we read that "Daniel purposed in his heart that he would not defile himself with the portion of the king's delicacies, nor with the wine which he drank." Because Daniel and his three friends took a stand in that relatively small area, I believe it gave them the strength later on to make an even greater stand. For Shadrach, Meshach, and Abednego it was a fiery furnace. For Daniel it was a den of lions.

That's why we all need purpose and direction in life. Otherwise you could end up throwing your life away. It has been said, "If you aim at nothing, you are bound to hit it." And a lot of people today are doing just that. The news these days is full of young celebrities who seem to spend their lives at parties and nightclubs, drinking, driving too fast, doing drugs, chasing sex, and basically throwing their lives away in an effort to fill that awful emptiness inside their souls.

For some men die by shrapnel,
And some go down in flames.
But most men perish inch by inch
In play at little games.[35]

More than counseling, more than rehab, more jail time, these young men and women need the Lord and the purpose and meaning He brings to every life that seeks Him.

We see time and again how Daniel was promoted in the two pagan kingdoms in which he served. But rather than trying to use his beliefs to win political office or get a promotion, it was because of his beliefs that his work, integrity, and character came to the attention of Babylonian and Medo-Persian officials.

Sometimes Christians will try to use their faith or their association with a certain church to get a job. That's backward thinking. Instead, because of our faith in Christ, we should be the most alert, polite, responsive, and hardworking employees wherever we are... and we will never lack a job.

Some people like to wear their faith like a neon bumper sticker, advertising their Christianity. People will put a little Christian fish symbol or a cross on their yellow page ad, business card, or letterhead. Or maybe you've given your business a name from the Bible, and so you talk to your Christian friends and say, "Hire me, I do a great job."

All of that is fine. But I would simply say this: *make sure you deliver the goods.* You should be the best at what you do—the best landscaper, the best construction company, the best air conditioning company, the best real estate salesman, the best attorney, the best whatever it is. You should excel at it. People should refer you to others not just because you are a man or woman of faith, but because your work and your work ethic are so exemplary.

That's how it was for Daniel, and that's how it should be for us. But if you enjoy success in your business or in your job, don't be surprised if you attract some envy and negative attention—as Daniel did.

The other administrators of the kingdom were angry that the elderly Jewish exile had been promoted—while they had been passed over. So they hired some undercover detectives to dig up all the dirt they could find on him. The problem for them was, there was no dirt on Daniel.

Then the other administrators and high officers began searching for some fault in the way Daniel was handling government affairs, but they couldn't find anything to criticize or condemn. (Daniel 6:4, NLT)

Motivated by envy and jealousy, these officials wanted to destroy him. Envy hates the excellence which it cannot attain. But as we will see at the conclusion of this story, jealousy will only end up destroying the jealous person.

I heard a fable of an eagle that was envious of another eagle that could fly better and higher than he could. So one day the envious eagle saw a hunter who had a bow and arrow, and he said to the hunter, "Take your bow and bring down that eagle soaring up in the sky."

The hunter said he would like to, but he needed some feathers for his arrow. So the jealous bird pulled out one of his own feathers from his wing and gave it to the hunter. The bowman pulled back the string and fired the newly feathered arrow, but it didn't quite reach the rival bird, who was flying too high to be bothered by arrows.

So the envious eagle pulled out another feather. Then another. Then another. Eventually, he had lost so many feathers he himself could no longer fly. "Hmm," said the hunter to himself. "Why bother trying to hit that bird way up there?" Instead, he shot the helpless, featherless eagle he'd been talking with and had eagle stew that night.

That's how envy works. Try to undermine or destroy your perceived rival, and you will be the victim rather than the object of envy.

Certain media outlets used to call President Ronald Reagan "the Teflon president." They said that because (try as they might) they couldn't throw anything at him that would stick! It just slid off, and the story would go nowhere. That was the frustration these bureaucrats had with Daniel. He was the "Teflon Prophet." All their usual sources had gone snooping in all the usual places, and they came up with a big zero. They couldn't come up with gambling debts, hookers, insider trading, tax evasion, or anything else.

But then someone came up with the bright idea of attacking his faith.

So they concluded, "Our only chance of finding grounds for accusing Daniel will be in connection with the rules of his religion."

> *So the administrators and high officers went to the king and said, "Long live King Darius! We are all in agreement—we administrators, officials, high officers, advisers, and governors—that the king should make a law that will be strictly enforced. Give orders that for the next thirty days any person who prays to anyone, divine or human—except to you, Your Majesty—will be thrown into the den of lions. And now, Your Majesty, issue and sign this law so it cannot be changed, an official law of the Medes and Persians that cannot be revoked." So King Darius signed the law.*
> (Daniel 6:5-9, NLT)

Clearly this was a smokescreen they were throwing up, and their real intention was to destroy Daniel. Just as they had anticipated, the king loved their idea. It flattered him, and he said, "Well, I would have never come up with such a law myself, but since you guys thought of it, I might do just that. It's kind of cool... . No one can pray to any god or any man except me. I like it. Where do I sign?"

So he put his signature to this irreversible executive order, never realizing that he was signing away the life of his friend. The effect of the law—at least as far as Daniel was concerned—was that he couldn't pray for the next thirty days.

What would you do? How would you handle it if a law was passed tomorrow by our government that said you could no longer pray in public for thirty days? Would you obey that law? If you were in a restaurant and your meal came, would you just skip saying grace? "Tell you what. Let's just pray with our eyes open. God knows our hearts. We don't want to get arrested!"

How easily Daniel could have said, "Well, there's no value in praying if I end up being put to death. How's that going to help our cause? I'll just set that aside for a month."

But what did Daniel actually do?

> *But when Daniel learned that the law had been signed, he went home and knelt down as usual in his upstairs room, with its windows open toward Jerusalem. He prayed three times a day, just as he had always done, giving thanks to his God. (v. 10, NLT)*

That brings us to a third principle we can glean from this man's life.

Daniel Was a Man of Prayer

It would have been a great temptation to shut the door, close the shades, and pray silently to God with his eyes open. After all, he would still be praying, wouldn't he?

But Daniel knew in his heart of hearts that changing his prayer habits to conform to this new kingdom rule would be a compromise. His sense of purpose would not allow it. Daniel stood his ground, refusing to be intimidated.

You and I will face similar challenges—not as dramatic as this one, perhaps, but tests nonetheless. Maybe it will be that prayer in the restaurant we mentioned. That's always an interesting moment, isn't it? Especially when you're having a meal with nonbelievers, you wonder, *Should I pray with nonbelievers present?*

I like to pray in a situation like that! I want to give thanks to God whether they want to or not. And also, when I pray, I have the floor! I get to talk and—for the moment, at least—nobody else gets to say anything. I'm not talking about praying around the world here. I just mean a few words of thanks to the Lord we love. "Lord, we thank You for Your love for us, and for Your provision of this food that You have given to us. We praise You for it in the name of Jesus, our Savior. Amen."

You don't need to make a show out of it and embarrass people. Simply take the opportunity to give a little praise and honor to your God.

Saying grace over a meal, however, isn't the only situation where people may notice something different about you and ask you questions. Maybe they will say something like this: "I notice you don't behave as everyone else does. You seem to work harder. You seem to love your family a little bit more, and they you. You seem to be so honest and ethical. And even though you don't party with us, you seem like such a happy, joyful person. What is it about you that makes you different?"

If you find yourself with an open door like that, don't let it slip through your fingers by making a bunch of generalizations. "Well, it's probably my upbringing. I was raised with traditional values." No, seize that opportunity to speak a word for the Lord. "Let me tell you why I am the way I am. It's because of my faith in Jesus Christ." Not to confess Him in a moment like that is really to deny Him.

Daniel wasn't going to do that. He wasn't going to back down, no matter what the consequences. He didn't change a thing when he was attacked for his faith, he just maintained his usual habits of meeting with the Lord and openly seeking Him. He kept on keeping on.

People may very well attack us as Bible-believing Christians. Being anti-Christian these days is one of the few politically correct hate groups you can belong to. People call us Bible-thumping bigots. They say that we are narrow-minded and intolerant.

But here's what it comes down to. We can't back down from what we believe. We can't hold back. We need to share the truth of God's Word when He gives us those opportunities.

Daniel's enemies had to resort to trickery and deception to get at him, because there was nothing in his life to accuse him of. We've all heard the old saying, but it remains relevant: If you were arrested for being a Christian, would there be enough evidence to convict you? If loving God were a crime, would you be an outlaw? It may sound strange, but I really hope that people who want to harm us would have to make up lies about us.

If you are truly attacked or slandered or mocked for being a believer—and not for simply being an annoyance or a jerk—then you have reason to celebrate. That means you're actually accomplishing something as a follower of Christ.

I like this paraphrase of our Lord's words from the Sermon on the Mount:

> *"Not only that—count yourselves blessed every time people put you down or throw you out or speak lies about you to discredit me. What it means is that the truth is too close for comfort and they are uncomfortable. You can be glad when that happens—give a cheer, even!—for though they don't like it, I do! And all heaven applauds. And know that you are in good company. My prophets and witnesses have always gotten into this kind of trouble."*
> *(Matthew 5:11-12, The Message)*

Just keep doing what you're doing. Keep praying. Keep telling others about Christ and living the Christian life. Don't let anyone or anything intimidate you.

Not only did Daniel pray, but He also gave thanks to God. Verse 10 (NLT) says, "He prayed three times a day, just as he had always done, giving thanks to his God." Now what did Daniel have to be thankful for? He had been harassed, insulted, lied about, and persecuted. Yet he knelt down every day—three times a day—and gave thanks to God.

We are commanded to do the same in Scripture. In 1 Thessalonians 5:18, Paul writes: "In everything give thanks, for this is the will of God in Christ Jesus for you." We are also told, "Be anxious for nothing, but in everything by prayer and supplication, with thanksgiving, let your requests be made known to God" (Philippians 4:6).

Yes, I realize that it's easier to thank God for past blessings than it is to thank Him before the answer to the prayer comes. But we are commanded in Scripture to rejoice and give thanks. And that is exactly what Daniel did.

Lion King

The king, of course, immediately realized that he had been duped by his devious administrators. He recognized what a fool he had been, but even he could not change the decree that he had authorized and signed. Daniel was arrested for breaking the new law, and he was well aware of the penalty—death by hungry lion. *At least if it's my time to go*, he might have reasoned, *the end will be quick.*
Scripture says,

> *So at last the king gave orders for Daniel to be arrested and thrown into the den of lions. The king said to him, "May your God, whom you serve so faithfully, rescue you."*
>
> *A stone was brought and placed over the mouth of the den. The king sealed the stone with his own royal seal and the seals of his nobles, so that no one could rescue Daniel.* (Daniel 6:16-17, NLT)

To me, the situation is almost humorous. There was a seal on the stone, as if that was going to stop God from working! Can't you just hear the God of the universe saying, "Oh, no. A seal on the stone!" Do you think things like this concern the Lord? They put a seal on the stone of our Lord when He was placed in the tomb after His crucifixion. That didn't work too well either.
We need to remember that any deadly plots hatched against us—no matter how well thought out or "foolproof"—will fail because we are going to live as long

as God wants us to live. A Christian is indestructible until the Lord is through with him.

Listen: when you die, you die, and you step into the presence of the Lord. If you live, you live, and you serve the Lord. It's a win-win situation. This doesn't mean we should be foolish or careless with our lives in a way that puts God to the test. But it does mean that we can trust God, knowing we are safe in His hands, come what may.

King Darius hoped for the best but feared the worst. He thought that surely his trusted elderly "prime minister" would lose his life in that lion's den. Scripture says, "Then the king returned to his palace and spent the night fasting. He refused his usual entertainment and couldn't sleep at all that night."[36]

Somehow I imagine that Daniel had a good night's sleep. Once he saw that God's angel was protecting him, he probably used one of those lions for a pillow. (*Leo, come over here. You have the thickest mane. You look soft. I'm sleeping on you tonight.*)

It wasn't because these were godly lions. They were very normal lions, even hungry lions. But none of them wanted to mess with the Lord's angel. And Daniel probably got a solid seven hours that night.

Real peace is being able to lay your head down on your pillow at night at peace with God. Peace is committing every detail of your life to the Lord. It is no longer being plagued with guilt. It is saying the words, "Lord, I trust You" as you drift off to sleep.

David, who had good reason for a lot of sleepless nights in his life, wrote, "In peace I will both lie down and sleep, for You alone, O LORD, make me to dwell in safety."[37]

I think Daniel could do that through most of his long life. King Darius, however, had experienced a rough night and hadn't slept at all.

Very early the next morning, the king got up and hurried out to the lions' den. When he got there, he called out in anguish, "Daniel, servant of the living God! Was your God, whom you serve so faithfully, able to rescue you from the lions?"

Daniel answered, "Long live the king! My God sent his angel to shut the lions' mouths so that they would not hurt me, for I have been found innocent in his sight. And I have not wronged you, Your Majesty."

The king was overjoyed and ordered that Daniel be lifted from the den. Not a scratch was found on him, for he had trusted in his God. Then the king gave orders to arrest the men who had maliciously accused Daniel. He had them thrown into the lions' den, along with their wives and children. The lions leaped on them and tore them apart before they even hit the floor of the den.

Then King Darius sent this message to the people of every race and nation and language throughout the world:

"Peace and prosperity to you!
I decree that everyone throughout my kingdom should tremble with fear before the God of Daniel.
For he is the living God,
and he will endure forever.
His kingdom will never be destroyed,
and his rule will never end.

He rescues and saves his people;
he performs miraculous signs and wonders
in the heavens and on earth.
He has rescued Daniel
from the power of the lions."
(Daniel 6:19-26, NLT)

I wonder if, as you read this real-life story of courage and faith, you find yourself in a lion's den at this moment. Or maybe you'd describe it as the middle of the fire, as with Shadrach, Meshach, and Abednego. Or then again, you might even feel like Job, whose whole world caved in. Like Daniel, you may have some enemies out there plotting your destruction. And you certainly have an adversary who "prowls around like a roaring lion looking for someone to devour."[38]

You feel like the heat's on, and you wonder if you can hold onto your sanity—and your faith—in this time of pain and perplexity. You look up to heaven and ask God what's going on, why these things are happening to you. *Why me? Why now? Why this?*

Daniel refused to be distracted from the purpose in his heart. He knew very well about the hatred and jealousy of his peers and their desire to trap him and harm him. But as far as he was concerned, those threats didn't change a thing. He opened the windows of his home to the sunshine and fresh air and prayed to the Lord three times a day, just as he always had.

He maintained his priorities and kept his cool in the face of opposition and intimidating circumstances. So did Shadrach, Meshach, and Abednego, when ordered to betray the Lord or die. And so did Job, when Satan stole everything from him but that which he cherished most—

his relationship with the living God.

These real people from the pages of Scripture teach us to keep our eyes of faith locked on our faithful God no matter what. Keep on praying... keep on living a godly life... keep on claiming the promises of God's Word... keep on trusting the Lord to come through for you and to continue working for your best and His glory.

We will certainly find ourselves in some hot, uncomfortable places as we live out our lives on this side of heaven. We may find ourselves in dark valleys of grief or pain. We may find ourselves in the company of lions. And we may even find ourselves crying out, "God, *why?*"

But we will never find ourselves alone.

Endnotes

1   Luke 18:19, NIV
2   Romans 3:4
3   The Message
4   Colossians 3:5, NIV
5   1 Thessalonians 5:17-18
6   Luke 10:18
7   2 Corinthians 2:11, NIV
8   Revelation 12:10
9   1 Peter 5:8
10   John 8:44
11   Luke 22:31-32
12   1 John 2:1, THE MESSAGE
13   Psalm 103:11-12, THE MESSAGE
14   Luke 22:53, NLT
15   Zechariah 12:10; Psalm 22
16   Isaiah 53:10, NIV
17   Zechariah 11:12-13
18   See Matthew 26:36-44.
19   See Ecclesiastes 3:4.
20   1 Thessalonians 4:13, NIV
21   James 1:2-4, PHILLIPS
22   Acts 16:26-28, NIV
23   John 9:2, NLT
24   Psalm 119:67, 71. See also Psalm 119:75.
25   http://unmuseum.mus.pa.us/hangg.htm
26   Romans 14:23, KJV; Romans 14:23, TLB
27   Philippians 3:10, AMP
28   2 Timothy 3:10, NLT
29   Hebrews 11:24-26, NIV
30   Isaiah 40:11
31   See John 10:3-4.
32   Matthew 28:20, NIV; Hebrews 13:5
33   John 16:33, NLT
34   Daniel 6:4, NLT
35   From the poem, "The Night They Burned Shanghai," by Robert D. Abrahams

36   Daniel 6:18, NLT
37   Psalm 4:8, NASB
38   1 Peter 5:8, NIV

About the Author

Greg Laurie is the pastor of Harvest Christian Fellowship (one of America's largest churches) in Riverside, California. He is the author of over thirty books, including the Gold Medallion Award winner, *The Upside-Down Church*, as well as *Every Day with Jesus; Are We Living in the Last Days?*; *Marriage Connections; Losers and Winners, Saints and Sinners;* and *Dealing with Giants.* You can find his study notes in the *New Believer's Bible* and the *Seeker's Bible.* Host of the *Harvest: Greg Laurie* television program and the nationally syndicated radio program *A New Beginning,* Greg Laurie is also the founder and featured speaker for Harvest Crusades—contemporary, large-scale evangelistic outreaches, which local churches organize nationally and internationally. He and his wife, Cathe, live in Southern California and have two children and one grandchild.

Other AllenDavid books published by Kerygma Publishing

The Great Compromise

For Every Season: Daily Devotions

Strengthening Your Marriage

Marriage Connections

Are We Living in the Last Days?

"I'm Going on a Diet Tomorrow"

Strengthening Your Faith

Deepening Your Faith

Living Out Your Faith

Dealing with Giants

Secrets to Spiritual Success

How to Know God

10 Things You Should Know About God and Life

For Every Season, vol. 2

The Greatest Stories Ever Told, vol.1

Making God Known

The Greatest Stories Ever Told, vol. 2

His Christmas Presence

Visit: www.kerygmapublishing.com
www.allendavidbooks.com
www.harvest.org